Praise for

Team Building for Financial Advisors

by Christine Timms

"I've read the *Team Building for Financial Advisors* handbook three times now, there is so much great content in this book!"

—Jennifer Jackson
Financial Advisor for over 20 years
Big Five Canadian Bank owned brokerage firm

"I really like your approach and, in particular, all the useful templates and checklists you provide. It is far more practical than many practice management books I have read over the 32 years I have been in the industry."

—Gary Mayzes
Senior management of a Big Five Canadian Bank

CT Financial

Handbooks for the Professional Financial Advisor

Team Building
for
Financial Advisors

*Enhance Client Services,
Grow Your Business and
Improve Your Life*

Christine Timms

Paperback ISBN: 978-1-7773145-0-7
French Flap Paperback ISBN: 978-1-7773145-1-4
ePub ISBN: 978-1-7773145-2-1
MOBI ISBN: 978-1-7773145-3-8
PDF ISBN: 978-1-7773453-4-1

Published by CT Financial Press

Cover design by CT Financial Press & Melissa Levesque

Edited by Kristen Silva

Refer to www.ChristineTimms.com to buy handbooks and templates from the "Handbooks for the Professional Financial Advisor" series

I dedicate this book to my mother, Marion Timms, who by example, taught me the benefits of treating people as I would like to be treated.

To this day, my mother continues to make all those around her feel valued and appreciated.

Contents

Introduction to the Handbooks for the Professional Financial Advisor Series

I see myself as a client advocate who believes the best way to help financial services clients is to help the advisors who give independent financial advice. For the purposes of this series, I will define a financial advisor as an individual looking to provide services relating to investments, financial planning and/or insurance to individuals and small businesses. I believe that clients are best served by continuous long-term relationships with human advisors who seek to understand and work with the client to achieve the client's goals. The following quote from a note I received from a couple upon my retirement confirms that belief:

> *"In wishing you the best, we want to thank you and your team for looking after our investments so well over the last 20 years. With a high level of professionalism, you have guided us through good times and bad with the consistent proven good advice to 'stay the course'. Throughout, you have communicated openly, proactively and reviewed and reported on our circumstances consistently. Not only did you provide guidance with our investment portfolio but also took the time to advise us in the overlapping areas of tax issues, insurance benefits, estate planning and will preparation. Lastly our yearly reviews were not only extremely helpful but cemented the personal relationships. Thank you!"*
>
> —retired couple

I believe that by helping advisors succeed, I will help financial services clients succeed. I am also hoping that management of advisor firms, regulators and industry product/service suppliers will read these handbooks to gain a deeper awareness of the uniqueness and needs of both advisors and advisors' clients.

A financial advisor's job has always been stressful due to the unpredictability of financial markets and the people issues of any service industry. I believe the job is even more difficult today because of increased competition, the expansion of potential services (financial planning, etc.) and the growing number of investments available as well as increasing regulatory requirements. The good news is that advisors who use constantly evolving fintech and processes to improve their services and efficiency are able to increase the capacity and profitability of their practice while making advice available to more people.

I have written these handbooks to coach and assist advisors hoping to help reduce their stress and increase their productivity. I present ideas and processes relating to all aspects of a financial services practice with an emphasis on services, organization and preparedness. Preparedness reduces the stress of encounters with clients, prospects, markets, etc. Having a clearly articulated business plan, sharing the workload with a team and having a succession plan in place all work to reduce the stress of the business while making it easier to serve more clients effectively and profitably. The ideas are intended to help all advisors regardless of their unique approach to investing and client service, their unique clientele and their practice size. I hope to make it easier for advisors to serve their clients well, to the benefit of all stakeholders in a strong, sustainable financial advice industry (clients, advisors, advisors' firms, product providers).

As you might expect, this means sharing my experiences from my 33-year career as a financial advisor and showing what I learned from my mistakes. However, it also means sharing many templates and calculators (downloadable from my website) to help advisors easily implement the ideas that I share. During my career, I attended many practice management seminars agreeing with much of the advice given, but failing to implement the ideas because it would take too much time to do so. I am going to provide templates and calculators using my practice as an example, but I fully expect advisors to edit, modify and customize them to match their personal approach and the needs of their unique clientele. My customizable templates will help an advisor implement the ideas quickly as it is much easier to edit, modify and customize than it is to create from scratch.

> *"I really like your approach and, in particular, all the useful templates and checklists you provide. It is far more practical than many practice management books I have read over the 32 years I have been in the industry."*
>
> —Gary Mayzes
> Senior management of a Big Five Canadian Bank

I have been asked if these handbooks are intended to be "best practices for financial advisors." I hope they are "good practices for financial advisors" handbooks. I can't possibly claim "best" practices as I know there are many techniques and processes created by many advisors and/or firms that I am not even aware of.

I enjoyed helping many advisors over the years, sometimes formally under a firm inspired mentor program and sometimes through seminars sanctioned by management. However, most of my mentoring was "ad hoc" primarily for advisors within my own firm whom I met at conferences or within my own branch. These books are an opportunity to provide more complete and thorough mentoring for more financial advisors with practices in all financial services channels ranging from the large bank dealer to the financial planner operating as a sole practitioner.

> *"I have been in the business for 25+ years working in various management roles. I have worked with many investment advisors in my career and must tell you from a 'client first mindset', Chris is one of the best. ... We could all learn a thing or two from Chris."*
>
> —Wilma Ditchfield
> Senior management of a Big Five Canadian Bank

Handbooks in the Series

As I write this introduction to my series of handbooks for financial advisors, I have essentially completed handbooks regarding business models, team building, and transitioning clients and the retirement exit decision. I expect to complete another handbook about presentations and processes in the near future.

These books will reflect my strong belief that the "win-win" approach builds happier, sustainable relationships with all the stakeholders of your practice (clients, team members, branch management, service/product providers and senior firm management). The win-win concept does not mean that you compromise your own benefits but rather you grow the size of the pie to be shared so that all parties receive more—it is winning alongside each of the other stakeholders of your practice.

I recommend reading the entire series of handbooks once even though some areas may not seem immediately applicable to your practice. For example, you may think you are too young to consider the chapters relating to retirement or transitioning a clientele; however, you are likely not too young to think about pursuing a group referral of clients from another advisor. An advisor approaching retirement may initially see no need to read the business models handbook; however, upon reading it, they will see how they can easily articulate and compare their business model to that of the appropriate successor advisor. I have provided a detailed table of contents in each book to provide a quick overview and to help you easily refer to specific topics as the need arises over time.

Business Models for Financial Advisors

> *"You have set a great example for others running a very strong and successful practice…. I always knew your clients were very well taken care of."*
>
> —Steve Geist
> Former Group Head - Wealth Management
> Canadian Imperial Bank of Commerce

A well-articulated, written business model is a valuable tool for advisors at all stages of their career. An Advisor's deeper understanding of their own practice and who it serves best, will lead to sustainable relationships based on a win-win business model. I will define an advisor's business model as the articulation of who the advisor's most compatible clients are, the services and products that the advisor offers those clients, how those products/services are provided, how clients are charged and how the advisor is paid. I show how advisors in all stages of their careers can benefit from a well-defined business model, even those about to retire. The handbook provides a checklist process to quickly articulate, develop or analyze an existing or desired unique business model. I provide an example of the process by showing completed checklists based on the final years of my practice and the resulting printed business model. I include discussions regarding many of the required decisions as we progress through the checklists for the various business model components. I also discuss household capacity of practices and provide an analytical tool and checklists to facilitate the segmentation of clientele. This handbook includes appendices "Why Advisors are Not Interchangeable", "Why Many Full-Service Independent Revenue Sharing Advisors Have and Deserve Above Average Incomes" and "The Average Advisor of Various Financial Advice Channels."

Team Building for Financial Advisors

> *"Chris always seemed to gather people around that seemed to know what they were doing, they were young and learning the business, but they always struck me as being competent. But more than that, they seem to recognize the interests of the client, and they look after the client just as well as Chris does. In other words, they reflected her."*
>
> —Dennis Dack (client of 30 years)
> Retired Director of Strategic Policy
> Advisor to the Chairman of the Board
> Ontario Hydro

My team played a huge part in my overall success. I believe that my business would have plateaued at about 20% of my final practice (assets under management and revenue) if I had not built a team. This handbook focuses on the benefits of team building, delegating, supervising, outsourcing, hiring, training, team structure, compensation, motivation, turnover, etc. Team building is another classic example of a win-win approach to business. All of the stakeholders in an advisor's practice (clients, team members, advisor and firm) win from the advisor's ability to work with and delegate to team members. My willingness to build and nurture a team allowed me to expand my service to existing clients and pursue more clients resulting in a bigger and happier clientele, which naturally produced more revenue to be shared by myself, my team members and my firm.

Transitioning Clients and the Retirement Exit Decision

> *"Chris cared and continues to care about her clients - absolutely evident in her approach to her team and her solid plan for her retirement and the transition of her clients to the RIGHT advisors. The final proof is her two successors' very high client retention rate three years after her retirement."*
>
> —Wilma Ditchfield
> Senior management of a Big Five Canadian Bank

I retired with the largest assets under management and highest annual revenue of my career. I believe this was partially due to high client retention in my later years as clients were aware of my succession plans years before I actually announced my retirement. Three years after my retirement the assets and revenue generated from the clients transitioned to my successors were higher than when I left.

The handbook contains three interrelated topics:

1) Seeking Group Referrals from Another Advisor
2) Transitioning Your Clientele to Your Successor
3) The Retirement Exit Decision

The need to transition clients from one advisor to another advisor can be triggered by many different circumstances. An advisor will make group referrals to a successor advisor when they are retiring, reducing their clientele or changing their business model. The key to a successful transition of clients is compatibility between the successor, referring advisor and the clientele being referred. I believe this compatibility is more likely to be achieved when the successor and the referring advisor understand each other's positions and business models. Reading all three topics will provide the reader with needed insight and understanding in addition to providing step-by-step processes and tools to complete the transition.

Deciding when to retire is a very personal decision. I give my own reasons in "Why I Retired" as well as what I enjoy most about being retired. In "Hints That It May Be Time to Start Preparing for Retirement", I have provided a list of possible reasons for retiring that I have experienced or learned from others in the financial advice industry. I then point out many of the personal and business dangers of waiting too long to retire. Finally, I outline several steps that I recommend in preparation for an advisor's retirement.

Future Handbook on Processes and Presentations

I have gathered much of the content but have yet to complete the handbook relating to processes and presentations. This book will provide a lot of the "nuts and bolts" needed to implement an advisor's business model. Our presentations and interactions with clients showed them that we understood them and their needs making it easier for clients to trust us and understand our advice. The use of systematic processes and templates by yourself and your team will enable efficient delegation and supervision of the performance of many of the activities needed to find and service your sustainable client base and help you run your practice. During my career, my team and I developed many detailed presentations and processes including templates, calculators and macros for all six of the business model components with an emphasis on the major categories of the service model. These processes along with a good contact management system (client relationship management software or CRM) allowed me to grow my clientele and expand both my team and services. This handbook will discuss processes and presentations in great detail for each business model component and provide tools and templates to help advisors easily implement and customize the ideas that appeal to them.

I hope these handbooks leave advisors with a lot to think about, some ideas relevant to their practice and the means to implement those ideas.

> *"I have found all three of these books to be very thought provoking, not only as it relates to the information provided, but also from looking forward within the context of my own practice and my own personal plan for the next stage of my life."*
>
> —Rollie Guenette
> Financial Advisor for over 25 years
> Chairman's Club member
> Big Five Canadian bank owned brokerage firm

Team Building
for
Financial Advisors

Introduction

My team played a huge part in my overall success. I believe that my business would have plateaued at about 20% of my final practice (assets under management and revenue) if I had not built a team. They were involved in every aspect of my business. My team provided timely and accurate client service and maintained good relationships with clients helping me attract referrals. They performed numerous duties that allowed me to focus on communicating with existing clients and pursuing new business. They collaborated with me in the development of our service model, approach to marketing, selection and monitoring of money managers, and the continuous modification of our templates, macros and calculators as well as hiring and evaluating other team members. Their participation gave them valuable experience and knowledge preparing them for careers in the financial industry. I am proud to say that many of my former assistants have gone on to successful careers in the financial industry. One assistant left my team to become a branch administrator and later became a compliance, regulatory risk consultant for Branch Management Teams. Another became very involved in the systems development projects for advisors. Several became advisors, one started his own investment firm, one started his own financial planning firm and yet another became a "mutual fund manager of the year". Two of them took over my practice upon my retirement.

In the beginning of my career, I shared an assistant with three or four other advisors. I was a professional accountant with only a few years' experience in the business world, very little experience in the investment industry and, more importantly, no clients. A very low assistant per advisor ratio is to be expected when you are starting out. You have to prove yourself worthy of the higher expense before you can expect your firm to take the risk of hiring extra help for you. When you are sharing your assistant with multiple advisors, you are only going to get help answering your phone and doing some administrative tasks. Although it may be frustrating at the time, the inexperienced advisor will learn a lot about the business by doing some of the administrative jobs themselves at the beginning of their career.

The use of assistants/teams in the financial industry has increased dramatically over the last 10+ years. When I was hired as a rookie advisor in 1983, almost every advisor shared an assistant with multiple advisors. Only the very successful and forward-thinking advisors had one or more assistants to themselves and were likely paying a portion of the salaries as well as all of the bonuses. Most advisors were uncomfortable with delegating and/or did not see the value that more assistants could bring to their practice. Over the years the industry has evolved such that teams are now considered to be an integral part of "best practices". I believe I was practicing for five years before I had one assistant to myself. The first step towards building a team is always the hardest step. The cost of your first 1:1 assistant is likely a large percentage of your revenue, and you may not be sure that you can delegate enough to make the expense worthwhile. The purpose of this book is to help advisors see the benefit of adding team members and to help you maximize your team's productivity.

During this book I will discuss:
1) Benefits of Team Building
2) Delegation and Supervision
3) Outsourcing to Access Specialists and/or Save Time
4) When to Add a Team Member
5) Hiring New Team Members
6) Training Team Members
7) Team Structure
8) Team Compensation
9) Motivating/Inspiring the Team

10) Team Meetings

11) Relationships with Team Members

12) Team Member Turnover

I also include "Team Member Duty Lists" for various team member roles in the appendix.

Benefits of Team Building

Team building is another classic example of a win-win approach to business. All of the stakeholders in an advisor's practice (clients, team members, advisor and firm) win from the advisor's ability to work with and delegate to team members. I have listed many of the benefits below, and I believe more will become apparent to you as you read the delegating, training and team structure sections of this book. I am sure you will discover many more advantages as you build a team unique to your practice.

Client Benefits

Accessibility: My team was large enough to enable us to answer clients' calls immediately (no voicemail) with very little phone tag. Many of our clients' comments during my career highlighted their appreciation for this service, for example:

> *"Your awareness of your client's needs is reflected in your providing a human response to telephone enquiries and ensuring that all calls are returned promptly. For this you are to be applauded. With other calls I make when I hear the machine say 'your call is important to us' etc. I often wonder why in hell they don't answer the phone, if my call is so important to them."*
>
> —excerpt from a client letter

Faster responses: E-mails and questions were answered by team members as soon as possible.

More communication: The size of the team provided the time for more update letters and more phone calls to keep in touch.

More services: We were able to provide more services to clients because of multiple skill sets of team members regarding research, financial planning, taxes and computer programs (Excel, Word, PowerPoint, etc.)

Multiple relationships: Strong relationships with at least two members of the team, including the advisor, gave clients peace of mind, knowing they would be taken care of by someone who knew their situation even if the advisor was unavailable in the short term or "hit by a bus".

Continuous service: The advisor and other members of the team were backed up when they were away for business or personal reasons.

Better advice: Including team members in the decision-making process, by allowing them to question previous decisions and to make suggestions of their own, resulted in better decisions and preparation for client discussions. A client told me he liked my use of associates because "two heads are better than one".

Team Member Benefits

Opportunity to enter financial industry: Team members are provided with an opportunity to enter the financial advice industry and determine if it is the right career path for them.

Experience: Team members gain experience while they earn industry credentials through industry courses.

Learn teamwork: They learn how to work in a team, including hiring and training others.

Back up: Other team members are capable and willing to help and back each other up during vacation, illness, periods of heavy workload, etc.

Career path: They are provided with a career path without leaving the team.

Train for advisor's position: As they progress, they learn how to be a successful advisor.

Many more team member benefits will become apparent in this handbook's sections: "Delegation and Supervision", "Training Team Members" and "Team Structure".

> *"My advisor was far more than a boss; she was my mentor. Her extensive knowledge and experience helped guide me not only in the position at the time, but in all my endeavours since. She provided me with invaluable tools: knowledge, structure, discipline, and leadership skills that in turn, enabled me to train and mentor others. Armed with these tools, I have successfully transitioned my role … towards projects geared to aid both advisors and clients alike."*
>
> —former team member

Advisor Benefits

Happier clients: All of the benefits listed under clients obviously benefit the advisor, as happier clients bring in more investable assets and are more likely to provide referrals.

Ability to serve a larger clientele: A team allows you to provide timely, quality service to a greater number of clients. The larger the team, the larger the capacity for more clients.

Improve presentations: Team members' observations and interaction with clients can lead to ideas on how to improve client presentations and answers to current common client concerns and queries.

Improve processes: The team helps create and implement processes (like those I will refer to in a future handbook about processes and presentations, some of which are or will be downloadable from my website).

Learn from team member knowledge and skill sets: An advisor can learn capabilities of new technology from their team. For example, I learned about Excel macros and to google "how to …" for various software programs from team members.

Expanded team capabilities: Some team members will have skills the advisor lacks. In my case some examples were website design, creation of graphs, creation of Excel macros and research tools (like Bloomberg and Morningstar).

Enables delegation: See section "Delegation and Supervision" below.

Frees advisor's mind: As my team assumed more day-to-day duties, my mind was freed to think about and pursue changing priorities. Over the stages of my career, my priorities evolved with the size of my practice, my investment strategy, my service model, my age, industry demands (compliance), industry opportunities (new products), new ways to serve my clients (financial planning, estate planning) and my desire to pursue new clients.

Good back up: My team backed me up while I worked from home for several weeks surrounding my giving birth to my son. The team gave me the flexibility I wanted for family life, vacations, etc.

Provides discipline: In later years I was responding to requests from associates to call and meet clients. My calendar was largely determined by my team after I blocked out days off and personal appointments. The contact management system combined with assistants meant I never had to think about what to do next, it was automatically planned out for me. I was determined not to be the bottleneck that slowed down client service.

Possible successor(s): An advisor's team might provide a ready-made successor(s) upon the advisor's retirement. This topic is discussed in depth in the *Transitioning Clients and the Retirement Exit Decision* handbook of this series.

Firm Benefits

More revenue for the firm: All of the benefits listed under clients and advisors obviously benefit the firm as the clients are better served and the advisors will produce more revenue for the firm.

Happier clients: Will enhance the firm's reputation amongst clients and potential clients.

Happier support staff and advisors: Will enhance the firm's reputation as a good place to work for advisors and team members and will reduce turnover.

Career path: Working in a team provides a long-term career path for employees.

Training: Provides a training ground for the future new advisors of the firm.

To build a successful team, the advisor must be willing to delegate and sacrifice time in the short term to train team members. In the beginning it may feel like you lose more time to training than you gain in productivity. However, training your team is really an excellent investment that will pay off in the long term. As your team grows, the benefits compound as your team members train and learn from each other.

Delegation and Supervision

"If someone else can do it, someone else should do it."

The Need to Delegate

I was only practicing for three or four years when I concluded, "If someone else can do it, someone else should do it." Eventually, I also concluded, "If you don't enjoy doing it, someone else should do it". I knew my time should be focused on doing what would impact my clients and practice the most. I also knew that it was very important that I enjoyed the time I spent working as much as possible. I have described the evolution of delegating in my practice in the rest of this section and some of the difficulties involved. In the interests of minimizing duplication, more specific details regarding my team members' duties are given throughout other sections of this handbook.

During my career I would often discover or think of great ideas and opportunities from conversing with a client or colleague, reading a book or attending a seminar. However, if I was spending all of my time and energy responding to the day to day needs of my clients, it was impossible to free up my mind to develop or implement the ideas. As my team grew, I delegated more and more of the day-to-day client service, giving us more time to explore, develop and implement my ideas.

I determined that my greatest enjoyment and the strongest impact on my practice came from communicating with clients and developing and implementing strategies and services that would help my clients long term. Eventually, I was happy to delegate and supervise just about everything else. I even learned to share my client relationships with my associates, so the clients could receive more contact, and my contact with them became more meaningful. I found that my willingness to delegate evolved and grew with my business.

Delegating is necessary to continue to grow your business, train your team members and maximize the use of your own time. However, delegating is not easy. I experienced many frustrating moments where I thought, "I can get this done quicker or better if I just do it myself". I had to remind myself that "short-term pain leads to long-term gain" in those situations. The cumulative compounding benefit of delegating should become more evident as we discuss what should be delegated.

What Should be Delegated

I began with delegating very basic tasks requiring very little knowledge or skill. After I became more comfortable with delegating, I realized that the skill sets of some team members made them better suited to some tasks than I was. For example, my Excel spreadsheet skills were somewhat lacking in comparison to several of my team members. I learned to work with my team to determine what the final spreadsheet/graph/document should look like and then I let a team member "make it so" (yes, I am a Star Trek fan). Today's recent graduates are most likely more capable in the use of most of the newer software programs/technology.

As my team grew in size, the capabilities and level of education/ knowledge of my team members also grew. Team members had earned their insurance licences, CFP (Certified Financial Planner) designations, CFA (Chartered Financial Analyst) designations and other industry accreditations. This knowledge combined with the experience of working with me and our clients produced financial professionals with valuable opinions and viewpoints that I would have been foolish to ignore. The team became very involved in our selection and monitoring of securities (stocks and bonds, etc.) as well as money managers (mutual funds and separately managed accounts). I was always asking, "What do you think?" regarding specific recommendations to clients. We would discuss the ideas put forth and the reasoning behind the ideas. As the team members gained knowledge and experience, I would find myself agreeing with more of their suggestions. I would gain confidence in the individual team member and delegate more to him or her with less supervision.

The sample team duty lists shown in the appendix reflect many of the duties I delegated to my team members in my last years of my practice as well as an overview of what the team spent their time on as a whole. The overview provides an opportunity to compare time spent with the intended focus of the practice.

Delegating Can be Difficult

Delegating can be very difficult to do, especially when you are just beginning to build a team. It is easy to delegate filing, letter stuffing and very basic tasks; however, to really take advantage of having an assistant, they need to do much more. Delegating means trusting someone else to perform tasks that you previously did yourself. I was always somewhat of a perfectionist and, in the beginning, found it difficult to let go of some tasks. More to the point, I found it difficult to let go of the "total control" I had over those tasks. However, as my clientele grew, I found myself bogged down with many necessary but unproductive and distracting tasks. I preferred to spend my time talking to my clients or developing ways to serve them better. This is when I decided, "If someone else can do it, someone else should do it".

Address Your Fears of Delegating

Some advisors won't share or delegate their relationships with their clients because they are afraid the team member will become an advisor at another firm and attempt to take clients with them. Some of my team members did become advisors at other firms; but, as far as I know, they never attempted to take my clients. Perhaps this did not happen to me because people were on my team for a long time before I had enough confidence to promote them to the associate role where they were trusted with client relationships. The progression of team member roles will become evident when we discuss team structure in a future section.

There is also the risk that the team member might make a mistake or error that costs you money and/or damages the relationship with a client. Yes, my team members did make the occasional error that cost me money and/or embarrassed me in front of a client. However, I believe that I was just as likely to make the occasional error as some team members were and that having a team allowed and motivated me to design processes to prevent and/or catch our mistakes. The fear of mistakes or oversights going undetected can be greatly reduced by the systematic supervision processes discussed below.

You can address these fears by revisiting the "Benefits of Team Building" section and weighing your fears against all of those advantages. If I had succumbed to those fears and been unwilling to delegate, I believe that my business would have plateaued at about 20% of my final practice (revenue and assets under management). I would not have experienced the same level of career satisfaction and enjoyment. Without delegating, I would not have had the time to develop many of the strategies and services that I describe in this book. I am also quite certain that my business would have grown faster had I been willing to delegate more and earlier in my career.

Making Delegating Easier

A good contact management system will be very helpful for delegating duties and client specific actions to assistants as well as keeping track of what has been done and by whom. The more processes, macros, templates and calculators the advisor creates for their team, the easier it is for the advisor and senior team members to delegate and supervise. A good template guides the team member through the preparation of the report/document and helps the member check their own work. Good systematic supervision processes will help the advisor catch most mistakes and allow the advisor to delegate with more confidence. My future handbook about processes and presentations will include ideas and examples of processes, macros, templates and calculators. I expect to make these tools available on my website to help advisors easily customize and implement the ideas that appeal to them.

Supervision

Delegating is wonderful, but an advisor is still ultimately responsible for everything the team does. The advisor must be prepared to oversee and supervise the delegated tasks. The degree of supervision required will vary with the business risk related to the task and the capability of the team member performing the task. Essentially, supervising/overseeing is reviewing the work to confirm that it is what you would have done yourself if you had the time. The advisor's practice's processes, contact management system and templates should be designed to minimize the time and effort it takes to supervise.

Systematic Supervision

The more systematic an advisor's supervision processes are, the fewer mistakes will fall through the cracks. Processes, macros, templates and calculators are the tools that simplify the supervision/review process because the advisor or senior team member knows exactly what to expect in the report/document/note, etc. with variations relating to the specific client's situation making it easy to check the team member's work. Consistent systematic supervision will provide the checks and balances needed to deliver quality control and prevent process deterioration. Systematic supervision also provides the advisor with indicators showing the need to modify a process, template, macro or calculator through the recognition of recurring mistakes.

— — —

Clearly, every advisor's practice is different, and everyone's clients are different; therefore, each advisor's delegation decisions will likely be different. However, I encourage all advisors to push themselves to delegate as much as possible. Keep asking yourself, "Can someone else do this task?" If the answer is yes, then you should probably delegate, especially if you don't like performing the task. Every time an advisor adds a team member, they will be adding to the ability to delegate throughout their team. The senior team members will be able to delegate some of what they do, freeing up their time so that the advisor can delegate more to them or work with them to develop and implement ideas for client service, marketing or practice management.

I think we have clearly established the need to delegate. It is now up to each advisor to determine how much can be outsourced and how large their team should be. You need to add a team member when you and/or your practice can benefit from the increased delegation enough to justify the cost.

Outsourcing to Access Specialists and/or Save Time

The first step of delegating is often accomplished through outsourcing. Outsourcing allows the delegation of tasks and duties without the commitment of adding a full-time team member. An advisor can continue to benefit throughout their career by accessing advanced skill sets beyond the capabilities of themselves or existing team members. In many cases, especially marketing, we learned from the specialists and were able to assume the task(s) going forward. I outsourced all of the tasks below during various times of my career.

Marketing
- Collaborate in the creation, modification and printing of paper, CD and audio brochures promoting advisor and various services (Today, I would consider outsourcing video production.)
- Set up and maintain website
- Prepare mailouts (stuff envelopes, etc.)

Technology
- Source, install and maintain hardware and software for office network, backup and remote access
- Source, install and maintain hardware and software for home computer and remote access
- Sourcing of tech gadgets, office machines and office supplies that are not supplied by firm

Miscellaneous
- Photograph, create, print or source printing of client Christmas cards
- Source, order and organize staff and client Christmas gifts

- Organize and host staff events and dinners
- Financial plans (My team assumed this task very quickly.)
- Record tax deductible expenses

An advisor will have to be careful to respect confidentiality of client information when outsourcing to people or organizations outside the firm. A spouse or family member can be paid for performing some "outsourced" duties (depending on their skill set), resulting in valid income splitting. In the later years of my career, many of the above duties were performed by my stay-at-home spouse resulting in income for him and a tax deduction for me.

When to Add a Team Member

The size of an advisor's team depends on the size of the practice, the practice's service model, the approach to investing and financial planning as well as how much the advisor wants to grow. Larger practices and more services usually require bigger teams.

Advisors have often asked me for a "rule of thumb" regarding the appropriate number of assistant/associates based on the size of the practice. As a result, I feel compelled to answer the question and will do so later in this section. However, I think the more relevant question for a practicing advisor is, "When should an advisor add a team member?". My team expanded one member at a time as the need for help grew. I did not add a member based on a "rule of thumb". My practice's need for additional help was driven by many factors relating to my evolving service model, approach to investing, desire to grow, etc.

Questions to Ask Yourself and Existing Team

I recommend that the advisor work with their existing team members to answer the questions below as they relate to their practice. Each "yes" answer could indicate that it is time to add to their team:

1) Are you or your clients unhappy with the timeliness or quality of your practice's responses to their needs and requests?

2) Do you find yourself or senior team members performing necessary tasks that feel like a poor use of time, or that someone else could do better?

3) Are you and your team so busy responding to the day-to-day needs and deadlines of individual clients that you are unable to do or think of much else?

4) Are you feeling overtired and/or in danger of burning out?

5) Do you and/or your team need more time to think of ideas to better serve existing clients?

6) Do you and/or your team need more time to actually implement the great client service ideas that you and your team have thought of?

7) Do you and/or your team need more time to think of marketing and prospecting ideas to find new clients?

8) Do you and/or your team need more time to actually implement the great marketing or prospecting ideas that you and your team have thought of?

9) Would you like more personal time but don't want your practice to suffer or stop growing?

If an advisor and their team answers "no" to all of the above questions, I expect the current size team is likely appropriate for the practice at that time. If you are answering "yes" to a number of the above questions, you are probably experiencing a lot of frustration. Adding another team member would likely reduce the frustration and boost your team's productivity. If you believe the need for additional help is temporary or seasonal or caused by short-term projects, (e.g., new documentation requirements), you could consider outsourcing a project or hiring a full- or part-time contract worker like a university co-op student. I often hired university co-op students on four- or eight-month contracts. They were relatively inexpensive, usually interested in learning and there was no long-term obligation. They were able to perform some of the simpler, repetitive, time-consuming tasks saving time for the rest of the team.

These questions should be revisited whenever you are feeling frustrated or overwhelmed and during your annual practice planning process.

Team Size Relative to Practice Size

The number of assistants an advisor needs will vary with the size of their practice as measured by the value of assets under management, revenue and the number of households. As all practices and advisors are different, I don't have a simple "rule of thumb" answer regarding the appropriate number of team members for a practice, so I will tell you my personal experience in hopes of providing you with food for thought regarding the appropriate ratio(s) for a particular practice. Keep in mind what you already know about my practice's client service model, approach to investing, etc. In 1996, 13 years into my career, my answer was about $40 million in assets per assistant. (Revenue was about $350,000 per assistant.) However, as the capabilities of technology increased, and my firm's systems improved, my ratio increased considerably. During my final years, I was happy with my team size of six full-time members (in addition to myself) plus one part-time member. When I retired, my practice consisted of approximately $400 million in assets, $3 million in revenue and slightly over 300 households. These numbers indicate ratios of approximately $60 million in assets, $450,000 in revenue and 50 households per team member. I did not increase the size of my team during my last 10 years although we were always looking for ways to be more efficient, and we did add many client services, such as financial planning.

When I retired my practice was still growing, but it was growing very slowly. We were accepting referrals, but we were not actively pursuing referrals or new clients. If I was still in a "high energy growth mode", I am sure that I would have hired another team member and spent more time asking for referrals and marketing our services. I might have had more time and energy to perfect several of my practice management and client service ideas while practicing instead of waiting until I began to write this book after retirement. Although the discussions of "rules of thumb" are interesting from an overall perspective, I think an advisor should add a member to their team based primarily on their answers to the questions posed near the beginning of this section.

Before you add a team member, you need to understand the costs involved and be confident that you will be able to meet the expense under different practice revenue scenarios. I never laid off team members because of bad markets. I needed the full team to provide clients with the necessary reassurance as meetings and phone calls with clients were often longer and more frequent during bear markets. The team compensation section of this book describes my approach to paying team members. The same section also refers to methods and tools for analyzing an advisor's potential costs as well as keeping track of actual team compensation costs.

Hiring New Team Members

A few years before I retired a client told me, "Your team works together really well", and asked me "What is your secret in hiring a great team?". I told the client that I hired inexperienced individuals, usually at the entry-level admin role, and did not expose clients to a new team member until they had proven themselves. I should have added that I involved my entire team in the hiring and firing process. In hindsight, my answer was an admission that I had made hiring mistakes but managed to protect my clients from most of those mistakes, so the client was not aware of them. Everyone makes hiring mistakes. Having said that, I still think a lot can be done to increase the likelihood of success in the hiring of new team members.

Hiring Process

Attracting the Right People to Join Your Team
In order to hire good people who will turn into long-term productive employees you must first attract quality, compatible applicants.

An advisor must identify the qualities needed for a new hire to become a valuable member of their team. Some of these qualities can be shown in the job posting. A quality, compatible candidate is more likely to apply if the job posting includes a fair description of the position's activities and the learning opportunities offered, as well as required qualifications. Other qualities will be explored during the rest of the hiring process. You and your team should be open and honest about everything the candidate's job will entail throughout the hiring process.

The advisor's reputation for treating team members fairly and for providing opportunities for learning and career growth will also help attract quality candidates, especially if the candidates are coming from within the firm.

Involve Your Existing Team in the Hiring Process
I would involve the entire team in the hiring process, and we would all agree on every new hire. There were times when my team convinced me not to hire an individual for all of the right reasons. In one particular case, some team members noticed a candidate's arrogance and questionable attitude that was more pronounced in my absence. Hiring as a team reinforces the team mindset with all existing team members and confirms that all their views are important. It also shows the potential new hire that you truly are a team.

The newest members of the remaining team were the most active in this process because we were usually hiring for the admin role. They had performed the role most recently and would therefore be the most involved in training the new hire. They would work with the branch administrator to sort through resumes to narrow down candidates for first interviews. Those first interviews were conducted by those same newest team members and the branch administrator and would provide the opportunity to discuss the actual day-to-day duties of the job. The associates and I would only be involved in interviewing the strong candidates. Nobody would be hired without meeting every member of the team, and every member had to be comfortable with the final selection. This ensured that every team member believed they would be able to work with the new employee and shared a confidence in the new team member's ability to succeed. It also meant that all team members were more likely to feel vested in the success of the new hire than if a new member of the team was dropped on them without the team member's personal input.

The new employee had the same opportunity to determine if they could be comfortable working with the team before they accepted the job. I have been told by team members that having met the whole team prior to their first day gave them more confidence and removed some of the initial nervousness. A more experienced candidate is likely to recognize the importance of having met the people they will be working with to determine comfort and compatibility before accepting the position.

Who to Hire as Assistants

Almost every member of my team started out in the admin role. When we added an additional member to the team, we would hire at the admin level and the previous admin assistant would be promoted to the assistant to an associate position. If we were replacing a member that left, once again we would promote from within the team to fill the vacated role and hire at the admin level. I believe that hiring at the entry level minimized the damage of our mistakes. The new hire, myself or my team would usually recognize the poor fit within a year or so, and the new hire would leave before they had much contact with clients.

I have listed many potential characteristics of a potentially ideal candidate. You should review the list for relevance to your practice and likely add a few characteristics I have not thought of to suit your practice and the position you are seeking to fill. It is very unlikely that one candidate will have all of these characteristics.

Attitude and Personality
- **Humble**: Willing to do anything that will help you and your team be more productive including filing, document processing, getting the coffee, etc.
- **Modest**: Acknowledge that they have lots to learn and can likely learn something from anyone
- **Willing to ask for help**: Ability to recognize the need to ask for help from others when required to ensure a client receives timely and accurate service
- **Respect for rules:** Natural, inherent respect for rules and regulations
- **Presents a professional image:** Suitable for a client facing role

- **Honest:** Naturally gives straightforward, truthful answers and is willing to admit mistakes
- **Integrity:** Are they predisposed to do the right thing and speak up when they think something is not right?
- **Curious:** A desire to learn and a willingness to self-teach through Google and YouTube videos
- **Cautious initiative:** Unbridled, unsupervised initiative can be dangerous, especially when they have data input and deletion capabilities.-
- **Common sense:** Need to be able to exercise good sense and sound judgment in practical matters
- **Personal intelligence:** In his book, *Principles: Life and Work*, Ray Dalio wrote, "Having an ability to figure things out is more important than having specific knowledge of how to do something". I agree but would add two words resulting in "Having the desire and ability to figure things out..."
- **Likes a challenge:** Not intimidated by being told to "figure it out yourself"
- **Ability to handle stress:** Ability to handle pressure caused by continuous and simultaneous demands from clients, team members and advisors
- **Follows the win-win approach:** Believes that everyone should benefit from a relationship (no losers in a good sustainable relationship)
- **Common interests:** Having personal interests in common with the team will likely help them fit in.
- **Enjoys people:** Enjoys constant interaction with people
- **Ability to empathize:** Ability to understand and share the feelings of another

Education
- We usually hired straight out of university/college, usually young and smart.

- Strong aptitude for the use of computers (especially Excel)

- University/college bachelor's degree preferred

- Canadian Securities Course (CSC) or financial planning course finished or in process, showing interest in the financial industry

- If hiring for a non-entry-level position, you should determine the specific education requirement(s) needed to perform the role.

Work Experience
- The tougher the better—possibly physical labor (restaurant work, retail stores, construction, farming, landscaping)—so they can appreciate how nice it is to have an office job versus most jobs and will have "toughened up" from experiences with customers.

- Financial industry experience might be helpful but not necessary (might result in bad habits and a "know it already" attitude).

- If hiring for a non-entry-level position, you should determine the specific experience requirement(s) needed to perform the role.

Looking at the lists above, it should come as no surprise that the "attitude and personality" list is by far the longest and is likely the hardest to correctly evaluate through a few interviews. In my experience, attitude and personality can often compensate for a lack of education and work experience, but neither education nor work experience can compensate for a bad attitude. It is usually better to hire the diamond in the rough than the polished "I know more than you" person. The collective experience and observations of your branch administrator and all of your team members will help to evaluate the personality and attitude of prospective team members. Even with all of this help, you can expect to make mistakes.

An experienced, successful advisor recently told me, "Good staff make your life easy; you need staff that put your clients first". I totally agree. I wanted a team of givers because I believe givers will put clients first. In general, we looked for humility, curiosity, common sense, people skills and determination along with a strong work ethic as well as a desire to help people. Our new hires needed to understand how crucial finances are to a client's quality of life and peace of mind as well as the client's ability to help their family and others.

Manage Expectations of Candidates

When you hire someone fresh out of university, they often don't really know what their long-term career interests are, and they may have unrealistic expectations regarding the duties of an assistant and that of a financial advisor. They might think it is all about picking the latest hot stock or predicting market trends, and/or they may expect to be giving clients advice immediately. I encouraged my team members to be brutally honest with applicants about the least appealing aspect of the job (filing, getting mail, documentation, etc.). We also discussed the potential for learning and advancement within our team and the industry. We would point to members on our team and successful former members of our team, who all started in the role the candidate applied for. We would inform the candidate of the initial compensation and potential for earnings growth. The candidate's reaction to the realities and opportunities was more important than their initial understanding of the job. A good candidate would be excited at the prospect of learning and very willing to accept the worst aspects of the job as expected and necessary. The sooner they learned and reacted to the realities of the job they applied for, the sooner all involved could determine the suitability of the candidate.

Potential Interview Topics

My most important goal of the interview process was to determine if the potential team member had the characteristics listed above under attitude and personality, although there was also a need to clarify the candidate's education and experience. I wanted to know if the candidate was more interested in what they would learn and how they would help clients reach their goals versus their starting salary. I found that using open ended questions prompted candidates to speak freely, hopefully opening up to provide insights into how they think, their likes, their dislikes, their values and their priorities. Some of the early interview questions should provide the candidate with topics they are familiar with to put them at ease and give them the opportunity to show confidence, preferences and priorities. The candidate's résumé and cover letter should help provide you with ideas for your open-ended questions as shown below.

Education:
- What were their favourite and most difficult courses?
- What was their most interesting assignment or project at University?
- What were their study methods (might indicate how they organize themselves)?

Technology Skills:
- Do they use Excel, Excel macros, Word and PowerPoint personally?
- What do they use the internet for—Google, Social Media, Purchases, Banking?

Work Experience:
- What did they like the most about the job?
- What did they dislike the most about the job?

- Ask for examples of angry customers or angry bosses and how they handled the situation.

Personal Experience/Views:
- Have they ever invested personally; and if so, what did they learn from the experience?
- Do they have any views regarding investment strategies?
- What do they do for fun?
- What historical or currently well-known person do they admire most and why?
- What do they read—newspapers, business books, biographies?

Personal Goals:
- What do they expect to be doing five years from now?
- What is their primary motivation/inspiration (money, intellectual stimulation, making others happy, other people's respect and admiration, family, hobbies, free time, vacations)?
- What do they find satisfying/gratifying?

Interviews should provide opportunities for the candidate to ask questions. They should be encouraged to ask questions about the advisor, the practice, team members and the firm, as well as the position's duties. The questions they ask will reveal their views and priorities as well as their level of interest in the position.

Warnings Regarding Hiring

I noticed in the process of hiring many people over the years that if I was replacing an employee who did not work out, I would likely find myself overcompensating to make sure that the person we were hiring did not have the same drawbacks as the recently unsuccessful employee. I can remember one instance where an individual did not work out for us because of his arrogance and lack of humility. He seemed to think he was superior to people who had worked for the firm for many years, probably because of his high marks and degree from a prestigious university. I have to admit that I was overly impressed by those marks when we were hiring. When we were interviewing the replacement, we found a very humble person with great people skills who, in hindsight, lacked the academic abilities to pass the industry tests required to advance within our team. The replacement and my team and I eventually realized he did not belong in our business, and we had to begin the hiring process all over again.

Avoid hiring applicants who come across as "takers, looking solely for self-benefit". Givers will naturally give better service to your clients and are better team members.

Over the years, I concluded that new hires should have no strong opinion regarding overall investment strategies, or their views should coincide with mine. A team member's significantly different attitude towards investing will be a source of ongoing conflict and potential team dysfunction.

Resist the urge to rush the hiring process. Hiring the wrong person is costly and frustrating for your entire team and possibly for clients as well. Take your time! If none of the initial candidates seem appropriate, interview more. No matter how good the first candidate looks, you should always look at more than one.

Training Team Members

Common sense tells us that through good training, employees develop the confidence and the necessary skills to enable them to perform their jobs effectively and efficiently with accuracy and speed. Employees need to be able to think for themselves, but it is a mistake to drop them into their job expecting them to "sink or swim" with little guidance. Doing so is unfair to them, your clients and the other team members who will likely have to clean up the errors. Good training leads to engaged, happy and productive team members who serve your clients well. I have found that the training/learning for a career in the financial advisory industry falls into five general categories:

1) Industry Courses
2) Review Advisor's Business Model
3) Technology and Software
4) Hands-on Training
5) Learning from the Experience of Others

Industry Courses

I insisted that all new hires obtain their securities licence as soon as possible and limited them to administrative tasks until they were licenced. I strongly encouraged them to obtain their CFP and to obtain their life insurance licence. After several years on my team, I encouraged team members to become registered as a discretionary "portfolio manager". I also encouraged them to take courses relating to options and futures for a deeper understanding of leveraged investment products, even though I had not recommended that kind of investment since my early years. In my later years, I encouraged the completion of more courses relating to estate planning. In most cases the courses were paid for by myself or my firm. The formal training and courses provided by the financial industry has expanded remarkably over the years and will likely continue to evolve. Reviewing the courses available is not within the scope of this book. However, I will say that credibility with clients usually increases with the number of letters after an individual's name. This is especially true for younger and less experienced team members and advisors.

Review Advisor's Business Model

All new team members should be given the opportunity to understand the practice's entire business model including who the advisor's most compatible clients are, the services and products that the advisor offers/provides those clients, how those products/ services will be provided, how clients are charged and how the advisor is paid. The details of the business model will describe the advisor's approach to investing and financial planning. The training for individual tasks will have more meaning if the trainee understands the purpose of their activity in the context of the overall business model.

Show New Team Members the Client Experience

An advisor should show new team members the client experience that their practice's business model service component provides. Many of an advisors' services are often evident in introductory meetings with prospective clients and in review meetings with existing clients. Our meetings with prospective clients included a detailed agenda, a seminar regarding our approach to investing, sample financial plans, reports, fees schedules, etc. I would review the material for these meetings with a new team member, especially our approach to investing seminar, giving them the opportunity to question and understand the reasoning behind our approach. I feel this is one of the best ways for an advisor to convey their business model to a new team member.

If you don't already have a written business model, my website provides a template using checklists and macros that will help you do so quickly. Further discussions regarding business models can be found in the handbook *Business Models for Financial Advisors* of this series.

Technology and Software

My team and I occasionally used online training courses for commonly used programs, such as Excel, and for my firm's in-house programs. Occasionally, software trainers' demonstrations at our desks were also helpful. However, I think we learned the most by simply exploring the programs' menus with our own database. The basics of our contact management system were easily understood through a fellow team member's quick demonstration of the most frequently used features. We also used the programs' help menus and encouraged team members to use Google and YouTube videos to discover how to achieve specific results in a software program. In general, we would teach ourselves and learn as the need arose. I often wondered if an advanced course in Excel macros might have been helpful for the development of some of our templates, but none of the advanced Excel courses we saw provided what we needed. Perhaps a course in Visual Basic (the programming language used for macros) would have been most helpful.

Hands-on Training

Academic course work is necessary and valuable; however, the knowledge becomes useful to your practice only when it is applied to real-life examples. Clients are people with unique situations that rarely fit into the neat and tidy facts presented in an academic course. Hands-on training is the next step that turns the employee into a productive member of the team. Continuous, naturally occurring, hands-on training will also improve productivity of an experienced member of the team when you delegate new tasks to them as their abilities and responsibilities grow. I will discuss what I have learned about hands-on training under the following seven topics.

1) Train Your Team Members to Train
2) First Show the "Why" and a Sample Finished Product
3) Tools for Hands-on Training
4) Encourage Independence and Self Checking
5) Supervision
6) Involve Team Members in Everything
7) Coaching and Mentoring

Train Your Team Members to Train

Hands-on training is particularly important when you do a lot of delegating. As the practice grows beyond yourself and one team member, the team member who last performed the task should become the trainer of their replacement as they move up within the team. They are the best qualified to train and supervise as they are most up to date regarding the details of the task. The trainer's confidence and sense of belonging to the team will likely be boosted by the added responsibility. However, those that are best at performing a task often find it difficult to teach the task as it is tougher for them to understand where the trainee might stumble and may have a tendency to move through the training too quickly. I am confident that our team would have enjoyed greater success if we had been more consistent with the hands-on training and if I had given more guidance to team members as they trained others. This section is intended to help the advisor and team members become effective trainers and supervisors.

First Show the "Why" and a Sample Finished Product

Where possible, the trainer needs to first explain why the specific task is done and show examples of the end result where possible. The "why" should include the benefits to the client, other team members and/or the advisor. If you have hired the right kind of person, showing them how even the most mundane repetitive task impacts other people, should motivate them to do the task quickly and accurately with attention to detail. Telling an employee, "Because we have always done it this way", is a quick way to dampen their curiosity and enthusiasm. Knowing the "why" also usually makes the "what to do" and the "how to do it" much easier for the trainee to understand and remember. The trainee should watch the trainer do a task and then perform the task themselves immediately, hopefully several times under the watchful eye of the trainer before being taught the next task. All team members should be constantly reminded that the completion of the task in itself is not the objective, but rather the objective of almost every task is to serve clients and to do so as quickly and effectively as possible.

Tools for Hands-on Training

Your team's templates and calculators will be great tools for training your team members. They will minimize the likelihood of errors and allow the trainee to work independently early in the training process, thereby minimizing the time required by the trainer. A good template is easy to follow even for a novice and should provide explanations and check points to detect potential errors. Some of our Excel templates would produce a red error message if a number was missing or out of balance. The consistency of the formatting provided by the templates will simplify and speed up the review and supervision of the work. I provide many examples of templates used by my team throughout this series of handbooks and on my website. I expect to provide guidelines for creating templates, macros and calculators in my future handbook about processes and presentations.

Encourage Independence and Self Checking

After teaching the basics, show team members how to find answers on their own by providing them with relevant contact lists and templates. Make sure the trainer is available for questions without hovering. The trainee should be taught how to self check for accuracy. They can check their work more objectively by looking at it from a different angle rather then repeating their own steps (e.g., checking a spreadsheet's totals instead of checking the input). Before submitting their work for review, team members should always ask themselves if their final product is reasonable in relation to the client's situation and in keeping with the advisor's approach. This self-checking will test their understanding and minimize the review time. "Getting it right the first time" will help the more senior members of the team make the best use of their time.

Supervision

Training should be constant and ongoing. An associate or I would review everything together before it was sent or presented to a client. The review was done in person with the team member who prepared the document/report/presentation. The in-person review was quicker for the reviewer and presented many opportunities to remind the team member of the "why" as well as providing quality control.

Involve Team Members in Everything

I am confident that involving the team in the process of developing templates, strategies and specific recommendations lead to a greater understanding of the work and the development of a professional attitude amongst my team members. Involving the team in choice of an investment or service gave them more confidence and conviction when discussing recommendations with clients. They were more engaged and brought a higher energy level to the team. The interaction from involving the team members also brought different perspectives and new ideas to the practice. I am confident that this involvement also resulted in better quality decisions. By the time I retired, I was involving team members in most if not all decisions.

Coaching and Mentoring

As a team member becomes more experienced and knowledgeable, their training progresses from being taught and supervised to becoming teachers and supervisors and finally being coached and mentored. My interaction with my associates was more like coaching and mentoring when they were in the final stages of preparing to take over my practice. It is important to keep in mind that an advisor's everyday actions and treatment of clients and team members is an example for other team members.

The following is a good example of hands-on training occurring naturally while serving a client through the combined use of templates, supervision and involvement:

My associate and their assistant would prepare for a client review meeting by using the various templates we had created for meetings: a Word document for the agenda, current investments spreadsheets, a fee spreadsheet, a financial plan, etc. I would review the prepared appointment booklet with the associate several days before the client meeting to remind myself of the clients detailed situation and to work with the associate on any recommendations. The associate would then finalize the agenda, the reports and the financial plan. The associate would sit in the meeting with myself (the advisor) and the client, participating and taking notes, etc. Members of my team have told me that it all comes together for them when they sit in the meeting and see the interaction with the client as the advisor goes over the meeting booklet with the client. They can see the importance of accuracy and the presentation format.

After the meeting I would often ask the associate to critique the meeting: Was the client happy at the beginning, during and at the end of the meeting? What did we do that worked well, and what could we have done better? What should we keep in mind for the future? Should we be modifying the template(s) for use in meetings with other clients? The associate would finalize the notes from the meeting, and I would review them for accuracy and possibly add some details. Once again, it is always better to have two heads instead of one. We maximized the learning opportunity for both the associate and myself.

Learning from the Experience of Others

Team members should be able to hear each other interact with clients and answer their questions while still maintaining some privacy. Junior team members can learn by osmosis (the process of gradual or unconscious assimilation of ideas, knowledge, etc.). Senior members can monitor junior members for training opportunities and quality control. I think team members should have the privacy afforded by sound absorbing cubicle walls that are high enough to require standing to see the person beside you.

Team members should be encouraged to listen to and observe other advisors and assistants for investment and practice management ideas. They may pick up good ideas for your team to implement, and/or they may learn about mistakes to avoid. I encouraged team members to attend branch and industry meetings regarding particular investments, etc. to broaden their knowledge beyond my own views.

Additional Team Training Tips/Comments

Emphasize attention to detail: Emphasize attention to detail in the beginning of a trainee's career—a good habit that will serve them well throughout their career.

"I don't know" is okay: Team members should be taught that there is no shame in admitting that they don't know the answer to a specific question. Acknowledge that no one is expected to know everything. The assistant must be willing to admit to clients, fellow team members and the advisor that they "don't know" and promise, "I will get back to you". This is a much better answer than fumbling through an inaccurate answer or pretending to know something they don't.

Install a sense of urgency: Install a sense of urgency by reminding team members that there is always someone waiting for their work, and no one likes to ask more than once. A client knows that you care about and understand them when you respond quickly to their requests and/or questions. A quick response to team member requests results in more efficiency and less stress for all team members involved by minimizing the revisiting and remembering of the situation's details. Every team member should take pride in giving a quick accurate response.

Curiosity is a good thing: Make sure all team members realize that curiosity is a good thing.

Avoid training for training's sake: Be careful to avoid training for training's sake. Make sure the knowledge and/or the skills gained will be worth the time spent for both the team member and the practice.

Mistakes will happen: Be careful not to humiliate the team member who is likely to feel most responsible for an error. According to one of my former assistants, my focus on preventing the error from reoccurring, instead of focusing on the individual, alleviated the pressure and helped her "feel like part of a real team".

— — —

The advisor and other team members need to be involved in the training of team members to create a highly productive team. The best training can be done naturally within the normal course of business (getting the job done for your clients while the training is taking place). I expect you will see many natural occurrences of training as you read my thoughts regarding team structure (especially the associate team structure). Much of my team's training was accomplished through the hands-on use of user-friendly processes and templates, supervision, and by including team members in many meetings and decisions.

Hopefully, the training ideas I have provided above will help you train your team more efficiently and effectively. I must tell you that sometimes it felt like I was always training someone and that training team members was slowing me down. I was frustrated by the time it took away from all my other activities, like client service, developing new ideas, everyday tasks, etc. Succumbing to this frustration is short-term thinking that will cost you more time and more production down the road. When you feel this frustration, (I would be surprised if you never did), refer back to the sections "Benefits of Team Building" and "The Need to Delegate". Obviously, you can't delegate effectively to an untrained person. Also remember that if you are training, a team member is learning. One of the common motivators of my successful team members was the need to continuously learn. If you don't motivate your current team members to stay with your team, you will lose them and the benefit of any training you have given them. You will be forced to go through the hiring process again and start at ground zero training the successful candidate.

Team Structure

The structure of your team is important in order to maximize the benefits of team building previously listed.   Your team structure must fit the needs of your practice (investment strategy and service model). The right structure will provide a clear definition of roles resulting in less confusion and greater peace of mind for clients, team members and the advisor. A good team structure will result in systematic delegation of most tasks giving team members more independence and autonomy. It will also maximize the productivity of every member of the team and provide career paths with opportunities for learning and advancement.

During my career my team grew from a partial assistant to a team of 6.5 plus myself. My team structure changed considerably as my practice and my team grew. I have listed what I believe to be the most common structures below:

1) Spontaneous or "ad hoc" structure
2) Specialist(s): advisor not sharing client relationships with team members, clients talk to multiple team members regarding different issues as they arise
3) Associate(s): specific team members (associates) are expected to build strong relationships with specific clients assigned by the advisor
4) Associate(s) with assigned assistants
5) Associate(s) with Specialist(s)

I have included a table showing when my team size and structure changed along with my client service model. I will also describe the "hows" and "whys" of this evolution, my frustrations and what I learned from the various team structures. I will review the value of including an assistant or associate in client/prospect meetings and the qualities I looked for in an associate. My "Team Duty Allocation

Spreadsheet" will show how the associate structure can work with small teams of one, two or three members as well larger teams. Finally, I include a section designed to help the advisor evaluate their current team structure and decide which team structure is right for their practice.

Team Structure Evolution

My team structure evolved extensively over time. I learned a lot the hard way and would now like to help advisors avoid my mistakes and perhaps skip much of the lengthy evolution process. Many of the previously mentioned client, advisor and firm benefits from team building were not fully realized until I reached my final team structure (associates with assigned assistants). I will show you the structures I discovered throughout my career in the order that my practice evolved. In hindsight, some of the evolution of my team structure was unconscious and likely affected or influenced by the evolution of my investment strategy towards managed money as well as the evolution of my client service model and the growth of my clientele.

Notes Regarding Evolution of Team Structure Graph

- Team growth was not always smooth through evolution. (Sometimes the replacement of a team member was delayed.)

- The group referral resulted in ultimately increasing the team from four to six members.

- We experienced less turnover after we reached the final structure.

- I never reduced the team (fired a team member) because of bad markets, even though our revenue fell by 37% during the three-year tech bubble bear market (2000-2003).

Outline of Evolution of My Team

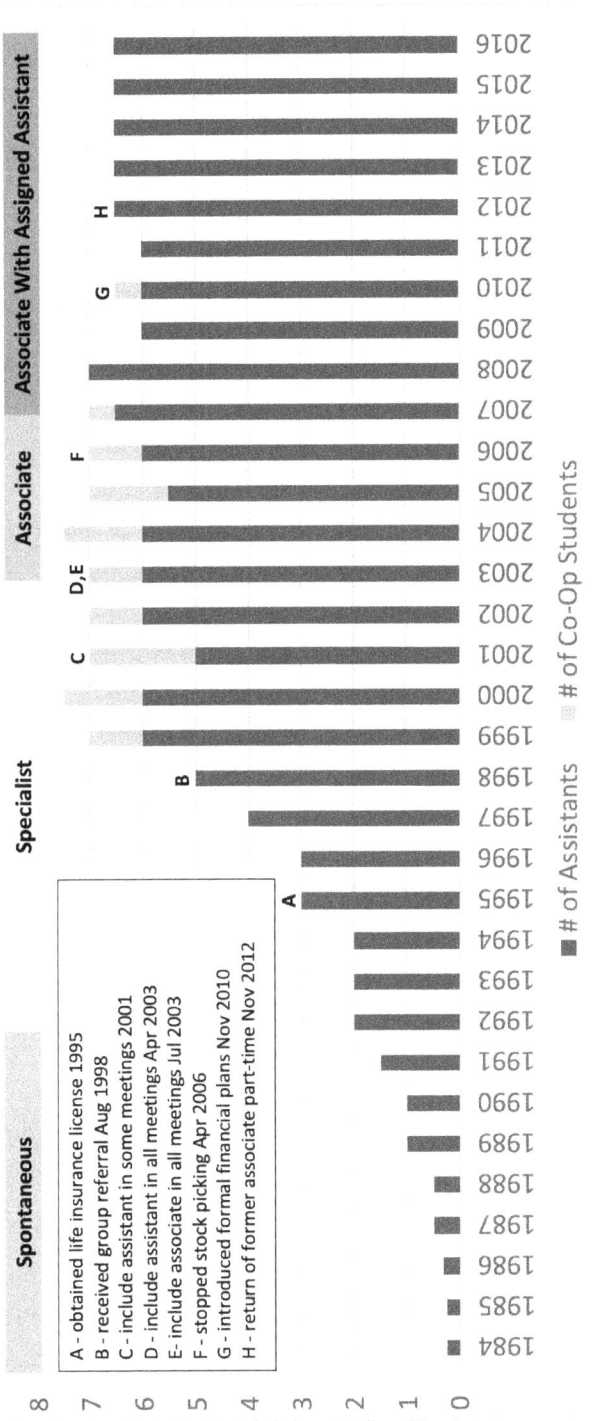

Spontaneous   Specialist   Associate   Associate With Assigned Assistant

A - obtained life insurance license 1995
B - received group referral Aug 1998
C - include assistant in some meetings 2001
D - include assistant in all meetings Apr 2003
E - include associate in all meetings Jul 2003
F - stopped stock picking Apr 2006
G - introduced formal financial plans Nov 2010
H - return of former associate part-time Nov 2012

A B C D,E F G H

1984 1985 1986 1987 1988 1989 1990 1991 1992 1993 1994 1995 1996 1997 1998 1999 2000 2001 2002 2003 2004 2005 2006 2007 2008 2009 2010 2011 2012 2013 2014 2015 2016

8 7 6 5 4 3 2 1 0

# of Co-Op Students   # of Assistants

Spontaneous or "Ad Hoc" Structure

Initially, I shared an assistant with three or four other advisors and the assistant only had time to help answer my phone and do some basic administrative tasks. After five years or so, I was beginning to understand the value of delegating and was therefore willing to pay to have an assistant of my own. I assigned tasks as they arose and continued to do so as my team grew. This unplanned, informal approach to delegation required constant improvising and continuous decision-making. I would now call this approach a "spontaneous" or "ad hoc" structure, which is really a nice way of saying very little structure.

Administrative Assistant

The administrative assistant role was established within this spontaneous structure and remained fairly consistent throughout the evolution of my team as we progressed through various structures. The admin assistant was an entry-level position for my team and almost always lacked experience. Essentially, it was their job to make everyone in the team more productive by performing tasks that did not require the knowledge or experience of the advisor or other team members. The administrative assistant provided useful services while they were introduced to the financial industry and the roles of other team members. Initially, they did not have much contact with clients other than answering the phone. They would also prepare documents, follow up on and solve administrative issues, handle the mail, do the filing and many other tasks too numerous to mention here. This lack of initial client contact protected clients from the mistakes of the inexperienced team member and from feeling the effects of most of the turnover on our team. (The admin position had, by far, the highest turnover rate on our team.)

> "When I was the newest on the team, I never felt bad about being the one getting the coffee because I could see that others' time was more valuable. I could see that if I worked hard and competently, I would be

moving up, learning more and the next new hire would be doing 'go for' jobs".

—One of my assistants who left us
to become a CFO for a small company
(and who remains a client to this day)

Specialist Structure

About eight years into my practice, my team members' roles started to resemble a loose specialist structure as I added people to the team. When I added a second team member, the newest person on the team was the administrative assistant described above while the more experienced assistant would perform duties that required some skill and knowledge but did not need me. They were licenced, would talk to clients about my recommendations, could execute trades and helped prepare for client meetings. This was the beginning of the research assistant role with occasional marketing tasks. There were no assigned relationships and assistants did not attend client meetings. I remember feeling, at the time, that I was spending too much time on day-to-day delegation, and I believe I fell into the specialist structure as an attempt to reduce the ongoing necessity to delegate each task and project as they arose. As additional team members were added, roles were assigned according to the assistant's capabilities and interests at the time the position was added. When I added a third member to my team, the research and marketing assistant roles became more defined while the admin assistant role remained the same.

Research Assistant

When I added the third member to my team, there was only a small number of mutual funds and no separately managed accounts available, so I was still building the equity portion of client portfolios by picking common stocks. After many years of stock picking, I had developed my approach to picking common stocks and determined what criteria I wanted to look for. I used, and often paid for, databased screening programs from research providers to identify companies that met my criteria thereby reducing the number of stocks to investigate further. I found that I did not enjoy the in depth reading that I considered necessary to determine which of these stocks were worthy of recommending to my clients. I also preferred to spend my time talking to clients. It was probably at this time that I decided that, "If you don't enjoy doing it, someone else should do it", and therefore decided to delegate the actual stock screening and reading of the research to a team member who had a strong interest in stock picking. The research assistant would bring several possible stock picks based on my criteria to the team and myself, and we would decide whether or not we would recommend them to clients. I would avoid a stock where a team member could not recommend the stock with confidence and conviction. The research assistant would also call some clients to relay my recommendations and execute the trades for both stocks and reinvesting matured bonds. The research assistant would help prepare spreadsheets for meetings and recommendations in addition to other spontaneous client requests.

Marketing Assistant
I added the third person to my team because I knew I was leaving a lot of business on the table. I had marketing ideas and projects that I was not finding time to pursue. The marketing assistant re-profiled existing clients looking for more assets and life insurance needs. They helped prepare marketing brochures describing our investing approach and service model for prospective clients. The marketing assistant would also call some clients to relay my recommendations and execute the trades for both stocks and reinvesting matured bonds. The marketing assistant would help prepare spreadsheets for meetings and recommendations in addition to other spontaneous client requests.

Estate Planning Assistant
I obtained my life insurance licence in 1995 because I believed that many of my existing clients could benefit from estate planning services in addition to our investment services. In time, I felt that I needed to add a fourth team member to be able to provide estate

planning in addition to our investment service and still grow my clientele. My most senior team member was interested in focusing on estate planning and life insurance, so I created the "Estate Planning Assistant" role for him in 1997 and hired a new team member at the entry-level position. My understanding of "estate planning" in 1997 is what I would call "Financial Planning and Estate Planning" today. We both thought that he could help us provide more services to clients and do more life insurance business by developing estate planning/insurance processes, brochures and presentations including needs analysis. The admin and research roles remained the same while the marketing assistant's profiling of clients for life insurance needs now fell to the estate planning assistant. Much time was spent attempting to work with spreadsheets and cumbersome financial planning tools that were far less efficient or effective than those available today, 20 years later. In hindsight, the creation of this position was a mistake. When this assistant left approximately a year after I created the position, I realized the role had not produced enough client service or insurance business to justify the dedication of a senior assistant to this role, so I combined this role with the marketing assistant role and continued with the specialist structure. Interestingly, I spoke to this former assistant who is now an experienced advisor with another firm and learned that he had arrived at the same conclusion years after he left my team. We agreed that estate planning/ financial planning services should be provided through the same individual(s) who is giving the client everyday investment advice.

Portfolio Development Assistants

During the period that we utilized the estate planning assistant role, I accepted a group referral from another advisor who was leaving the business. This group referral is discussed in greater detail in the *Transitioning Clients and the Retirement Exit Decision* handbook of this series. This group referral increased my clientele's assets under management by 50%. In order to maintain our level of service for all clients, my team grew to six assistants including two team members who were described to clients as "Portfolio Development Assistants".

These assistants would prepare many of our customized spreadsheets and documents. In hindsight, this role was not defined enough because their tasks were still assigned on an ad hoc basis by me through our contact management system.

Including an Assistant in Client/Prospect Meetings

Two to three years after I received the group referral from the advisor leaving the business, I attended a seminar where the speaker said he included assistants in his client meetings to take notes. He was looking to shorten the meetings, save his time and protect himself from baseless lawsuits. I decided to include an assistant in meetings with a few of my larger clients, primarily so I could focus on the client and leave the note taking to the assistant.

A few years after I started to include assistants in some meetings, I had a meeting by myself with a relatively small client of many years and her new fiancée. A few moments into the meeting, it became clear to me that the fiancée was trying to convince my client that she should claim that her unrealized losses on some securities were somehow my fault and that she should be reimbursed for those losses. My client was very reluctant to go along with him, and she denied all of his accusations against me. Nothing came of it other than the client eventually transferred out to a discount broker. I remember the relief I felt when we received the transfer out notice because she was thinking about giving power of attorney to her fiancée, and I did not want to deal with him. However, the incident forced me to recognize how vulnerable advisors are to a client's false accusation. I decided that all future appointments would include an assistant to take notes and act as a witness. The mere presence of an assistant would greatly reduce the likelihood of false accusations, and the assistant's notes would also serve as backup.

Gradually, the experience of watching clients and assistants in these meetings pushed me to understand that all participants could benefit in many additional ways from the inclusion of an assistant in all client meetings.

Benefits from including an assistant in client/prospect meeting:

- The advisor is more focused on the client during the meeting, not worried about forgetting details (improved client service, advisor efficiency and advisor peace of mind).

- The assistant can carry out agreed upon actions after the meeting without needing further instruction from the advisor (improved client service and team efficiency).

- Clients become more comfortable with the assistant's direct contact when following up actions decided upon in meetings, as well as future contacts regarding other issues (improved client service and advisor efficiency).

- The presence of an assistant and their notes provides protection from dishonest clients.

- The assistant learns from the interaction between the client and the advisor (training).

- The assistant would often remind us of issues or remember issues raised by the client, ensuring that I did not have to remember everything about everything.

- Better notes are created. (I reviewed and edited assistant's notes confirming modifications and additions with assistant).

> *"Per your advice, I have started having an assistant in every meeting. It has been a relief to not have to do the notes and remember everything that was said."*
> —an advisor who has referred to me as his mentor

I recommend that you include an assistant in your client meetings as soon as possible (likely as soon you have an assistant to yourself).

Overall, these initial benefits saved me time, provided many good learning experiences for the assistants and resulted in better service to the clients. Including the assistants in the meetings with clients allowed me to see many clients' willingness to maintain a relationship with a member of my team in addition to myself.

Frustrations with My Specialist Structure
I was still feeling that I was spending too much time on the day-to-day organization and delegation of tasks. A lot of duties did not fall into the categories of research or marketing. I had to decide which assistant would prepare each spreadsheet or document each time I needed one for a particular client. I also had to choose an assistant to prepare for and/or attend each appointment with a client. We had to create call lists dividing the clientele amongst assistants every time we needed to contact a group of clients (call for retirement plan contributions, change a stock or mutual fund position, etc.). I gave one assistant the job of calling all clients to reinvest proceeds from matured bonds. I tried to ensure the workload was fairly distributed amongst team members by developing a very large spreadsheet where we allocated all of the tasks we could think of among team members and attempted to estimate how much time each team member spent on each task. The spreadsheet would be revised as often as every six months as our client service model evolved and as team member roles changed. Cross-training amongst the roles was difficult but necessary so that client service and team efficiency was not adversely affected by vacations or turnover.

As our clientele grew, it became more difficult for all of us to recall details regarding all the individual client's circumstances. Some clients were telling me they did not know who to call when they knew they did not need me for a particular issue. Some clients started asking for the same assistant they spoke to the last time they called in, and some actually asked to be assigned to a particular assistant. They were clearly yearning for more personal continuity and familiarity with members of my team. I began to realize that I was creating call lists based on which assistant knew the client best. I was also beginning to include assistants in all client meetings and began to realize they would be more helpful in meetings and preparation for the meetings if they had more regular contact with the specific client. The need to solve these issues and inefficiencies led to the natural evolution into the associate structure.

Associate Structure

I was almost 20 years in the business before all of the above frustrations with my "specialist structure" plus what I learned from including an assistant in client meetings led me to establish an associate structure for my team. This was probably the most important decision I ever made regarding team structure. I assigned each and every client household to one of my three senior assistants, who I began to call "associates". I was still picking stocks for a small number of my clients, so most of those clients were assigned to the associate who had been the research specialist and who continued to work with me to pick stocks. The associate shared their assigned household relationships with me and became responsible for the day-to-day client services as well as attending and preparing for client meetings. The associates would prepare and collect the necessary information to allow me to make quick decisions which the associates would then implement. I also decided that the growth in my business should come primarily from gathering additional assets from existing clients and their referrals. I believed such growth would occur naturally from giving better and more service rather than from chasing cold prospective clients, so less marketing was needed. Some associates were still assigned to some "specialized" duties/projects related to research, marketing, technology, etc. based on their capabilities and interests in addition to taking care of their assigned clientele. The admin assistant duties remained the same, and the other team members provided assistance to the associates and myself on an ad hoc basis.

It is important to recognize that I never gave up the relationship with the client and was sure to make contact during big events or changes in clients' lives. A large part of my days were spent in client appointments (4-6 appointments per week, usually 1-2 hours long) and on phone calls with clients. One of my former team members, who is now an experienced advisor with another firm, recently mentioned to me that he "felt our team worked well because we gave clients the option to work with other team members without removing access to you".

The associates developed a more thorough understanding of their assigned clients' situations. It was easier for clients to trust advice coming from an associate they spoke to regularly, making clients less dependent on me for day-to-day adjustments. The associate structure better reflected our holistic approach to client portfolios, and individual decisions would no longer appear isolated because the same person called with every portfolio adjustment. This structure was also very helpful as we progressed through various service models, some of which were brought about by our continuously evolving business (separately managed accounts, fee-based accounts, discretionary fee-based accounts). The associate was well prepared to identify clients who could and should take advantage of new service models.

As you can see, everything the associate does, prepares them to back up the advisor and possibly to become an advisor. It became very clear to me over the years that not every associate aspires to become an advisor. Many are happy to spend their entire career in the associate's role.

A few years into the associate structure one of the associates left. I promoted one of my portfolio development assistants to a junior associate who served smaller and/or simpler households and did not delegate any work except admin. The more senior associates took over the more complicated relationships of the departing associate. On two later occasions, I lost a senior associate, and the third associate stepped into the senior associate position with very little additional training. Another third associate determined that she did not want to be an associate or an advisor long term. This associate has moved on to a successful career within our firm and continues to keep in touch with me.

The problem of day-to-day organization and delegation of tasks was finally solved, from my point of view, as most of the duties related to particular clients were, therefore, naturally and automatically given to the assigned associate. However, the problem was not fully solved until I assigned the remaining assistants as assistants to specific associates a few years later.

Including an Associate in Client/Prospect Meetings
The sharing of the client relationship allowed my associates to focus on roughly a third of my clientele and gave them an in-depth understanding of the client's situation. As a result, the associate was more capable of adding value during the meetings compared to an assistant who did not share the relationship and was just taking notes.

Benefits from including an associate in client/prospect meetings:

- All of the benefits previously mentioned under "Including an assistant in client/prospect meetings" continue to apply.

- The associate's in-depth knowledge of the clients resulted in faster and more thorough preparation of the client's appointment agenda and booklet, often with the help of an assistant, and quicker pre-appointment reviews with the advisor (improved client service, practice efficiency).

- The associate sees the value of the preparation for the meetings (training).

- The associate sees how the advisor handles client questions during the meeting (training).

- An associate may know more details of the accounts than the advisor and will sometimes be better able to answer particular questions from a client, especially if the advisor has multiple associates and a large clientele (improved service to client).

- The associate's participation in meetings strengthens the client-associate relationship and builds the client's confidence in the associate leading to more comfortable direct communication in the future (improved client comfort).

- The interaction between the associate and advisor during the meeting shows the client that you are truly a team and that they have at least two knowledgeable professionals working directly for them (improved client comfort).

- Hearing the same message from two different professionals, often presented in two different ways, increases the client's confidence in the advice (improved client comfort).

- The interaction between the advisor and associate can show the client how much the advisor trusts and defers to the associate strengthening the associate's credibility with the client (improved client comfort/confidence).

- The associate feels like a more valuable member of the team … and they are more valuable from the experience gained (team building/training).

- These meetings prepare the client and associate for future transitioning upon the advisor's retirement. For years before I retired, I told clients during appointments that the associate at the meeting would take over from me if I was hit by a bus. The underlying message was that the associate would be there for them when I retired. This really paid off when I announced my retirement. Many clients said how grateful they were that they already knew and trusted my successor. My successors' teams were comprised of my team members. This was a win-win for all concerned—clients, successors, my team members and the firm (improved client comfort).

> "I am definitely getting more comfortable on the phone after sitting in the client meetings."
>
> —a team member promoted to
> associate by one of my successors

Associate(s) with Assigned Assistant(s) Structure

The final adjustment to my team structure came when I assigned one of the portfolio development assistants to each of my two most senior associates. The administrative assistant's role remained unchanged. The junior associate continued to do all of the work for their assigned clients except admin.

Many of the tasks relating to services, reports, appointment preparation and financial plans, etc. could be delegated to the assistants to the associates and supervised by the associates. Everything the "assistant to the associate" did, prepared them to back up the associate and trained them for the associate position. For example, inputting and running the financial planning program for various scenarios was a wonderful opportunity to learn about the short- and long-term impact of savings, spending, returns on investments and different financial planning decisions.

We last updated the duties spreadsheets in 2010, two years after the previous update, whereas previously we had been updating it every six months or so. Note that 2010 is two or three years after we adopted the associate(s) with assigned assistant(s) structure. I believe the need for these duties spreadsheets evaporated with the associate(s) with assigned assistant(s) structure because duty delegation became more natural (intuitive).

Eventually long-time associates would take some simple review appointments without me when we knew the associate's relationship with the client was solid. I would usually ask the client's permission to do so. I would go over the review appointment's agenda, the reports and the financial plan with the associate before their meeting. The associate's attendance and participation in many previous client meetings prepared them and the client for meetings without me. The assigned assistant to the associate would attend the meeting performing the same function as the associate would in my meetings thereby accruing all of the same benefits that the associate did from participating in client meetings with me.

Meetings with a Family's Next Generation (Under 30? Just Getting Started?)
The associate for the parents would often take the meetings with the next generation without me, often with the assistant to the associate. The next generation would likely relate better with the

associate because they were closer in age and could start building the relationship.

The Flexibility of an Associate Structure

Every team is full of unique skill sets and personalities. The associate team structure is flexible enough to allow you to acknowledge and utilize the skills and interests of different team members with thoughtful delegation of projects and assignment of clients. For example, the development of unique spreadsheets with many macros may appeal to one team member whereas the development of a website and marketing materials may interest another. The associate with the most interest in financial planning could be assigned the clients who have the most complicated financial plans. A stock picking advisor may have an associate who works on stock picking and is therefore assigned the clients who want more detailed explanations regarding stock selections. The associate structure is also easily modified to allow an advisor to combine the admin role with the assistant to the associate role when the newest member of the team is capable of more.

Integration of Specialist Role into the Associate Structure

Although the previous discussions show my preference for the associate structure, I do believe that in some practices, specialists may be needed to provide an expertise not available in, or difficult to develop in, other team members. Also, a practice may have duties that can and should be performed by one team member for the benefit of all team members. (The use of an administrative assistant is a great example of this.) The advisor will have to decide if they need to dedicate a team member to those duties/specialties or if an associate or assistant to the associate can provide the service or specialist expertise to the team while continuing to serve assigned clients. One could argue that the administrative assistant role that remained consistent throughout the evolution of my team is a specialist, in which case you could describe my team's structure as associates with a specialist.

I realize that some advisors have been very successful with a pure specialist structure. However, I expect that those advisors and teams would be even more successful and less stressed with an associate structure where the team includes both associates and specialists or where the specialist roles are distributed amongst the associates. I think the associate structure reflects a more holistic approach to the client and that a dedicated specialist should only be on a team that already includes at least one associate. I think clients and advisors need and appreciate associates more than specialists on an everyday basis.

Qualities I Looked for in Associates

Upon introduction of the associate structure, I expected associates to develop relationships with the clients I assigned to them. I looked for the following qualities in my associates in addition to the attributes listed in the "Attitude and Personality" section of this book's "Who to Hire as Assistants":

- Experience: Several years of relevant experience serving clients in our industry.
- Knowledge: Completed courses in addition to basic licencing requirements.
- Respect: I needed to know that they really respected me, my clients, my practice and the rest of my team.
- Commitment: They agreed and were committed to my approach to investing and the goals of our service model.
- Progressive mind-set: They had a desire to grow and a willingness to evolve the practice (always looking for ways to invest and serve clients better).
- Communication skills: They had the ability to explain ideas in layman terms both verbally and in writing.
- They trusted me: I wanted my associates to trust me enough to feel comfortable questioning my reasoning or judgment relating

to everything to do with my practice (investments, service model and processes as well as particular client issues).

- I trusted them: Obviously, I needed to believe that the associate would not attempt to take my clients to another firm or make recommendations contrary to my approach.

Finding someone with the above qualities is easiest when they come from your team as you will have had time to get to know them, their attitude, work ethic, etc. There is always going to be a risk, but I felt that the benefits for everyone outweighed the risks.

Clients, Team, Advisor and Firm All Benefit from Associate Structure

Many of the benefits below may be listed under benefits of having a team but were not there until we evolved to the associate with assigned assistant structure.

Client Benefits
- Clients now knew which member of the team to call for all their concerns.
- Clients felt less vulnerable when I was not in the office.
- An associate felt a greater sense of urgency responding to client needs because they had the 1:1 relationship with the client and were more likely to see clients as people, not accounts.
- The advisor and associates had well prepared backups, so client requests were usually resolved without waiting for their return from meetings, conferences, vacation, etc.
- Clients often built a relationship with the associate's assistant.

> *"Clients respond positively to the 'associate' title; it sounds more professional and indicates that the advisor is extending more trust to the team member."*
>
> —a former associate

Team Member Benefits

–   This structure provided a career path for the assistants within the team.

–   Assistants could realistically aspire to becoming an associate, and an associate could aspire to becoming an advisor. The associate could aspire to receiving a group referral of a portion of the clientele upon the retirement or downsizing of the team's lead advisor.

–   Each team member had very capable backups when they were away, and the returning team member (including myself) could catch up very quickly after an absence.

–   Team members were exposed to all aspects of the practice (good training for future opportunities in our team and/or industry).

–   The associate structure resulted in natural cross-training and understanding for each other's difficulties and contributions. This understanding naturally fostered more patience and willingness to help each other.

> *"The hardest part of the job is earning clients' respect and trust, doing so is easier when you are an associate and can focus more deeply on the clients you are assigned. Even rolling a bond was much tougher before I had the associate role; clients would ask more questions and did not trust me because we only spoke once or twice a year. After the associate role was established, relationships were developed through more frequent contact and participation in appointments. Clients began to readily agree to the recommendations I presented because they knew and trusted me."*
>
> —one of my associates who was on my team
> for both the specialist and associate structures

Advisor Benefits

–   My time and my associates' time were well leveraged and used more effectively.

–   Delegation of tasks became more natural and intuitive and, therefore, less time-consuming.

–   I had more time for personal client contact and to develop our service model and processes to keep up with the constantly evolving industry demands and opportunities.

–   I was free to take more time away from the office for conferences, due diligence visits and personal time off.

–   Team members had the ability to advance within the team allowing me to keep ambitious team members longer (lower team member turnover).

–   It was easy to promote from within the team for all non-entry-level positions, avoiding the morale killing situation of hiring from outside the team for roles above existing team members.

–   I usually had a ready-made trainer for new hires (the team member who last did the job).

–   This structure provided two extremely able successors to take over my practice when I was ready to retire.

–   If my associates had been unwilling to take over my clientele upon my retirement, a non-team member successor could have absorbed my team to provide continuity for clients improving the probability of a smooth transition.

–   All of these benefits resulted in reduced overall stress for the advisor.

Clearly, everyone benefited from the associate structure: clients, team members, myself (the advisor) and the firm.

Lessons I Learned from the Evolution of My Team Structure

The evolution of my team structure was driven primarily by my ambition to grow and serve clients better. My strong aversion to inefficiencies and my desire to maximize the entire team's productivity meant that we were always looking for ways to do things better. Most of my ideas to modify the structure came to me from client comments and a willingness to constantly re-evaluate everything I was doing. Looking back at the evolution of my team I can see that I learned the following lessons:

- The bigger my team became, the more important the team structure became.

- The structure needs to facilitate intuitive logical delegation.

- Well-defined roles should be understood by both team members and clients.

- Team members familiarity with and understanding of each other's roles breeds natural respect.

- An advisor's team structure and resulting distribution of team member duties needs to be flexible enough to provide backup for every team member, adapt to staff turnover and respond to the circumstances of the day (clients' evolving needs and stock market performance, etc.).

- A good team structure provides a natural career path and opportunities to learn within the team resulting in less team member turnover.

- A good contact management system shared by your team is needed to facilitate effective delegation and organize duties by both the user and the client.

- The associate structure was a huge advantage as I prepared for retirement and transitioning my clientele to my successors.

I learned a lot of these lessons the hard way. I hope that this discussion and the section below will help advisors develop the best team structure for their practice while avoiding my mistakes and much of my lengthy team structure evolution process.

Which Team Structure is Right for Your Practice?

Every advisor should consciously decide on the structure of their team as soon as they have one or more team members dedicated to their practice. I evolved through most of the structures mentioned at the beginning of this section and have concluded that an associate structure is best for most practices. Although, I had a large team of six assistants before I adopted an associate structure, I believe an advisor can implement a form of the associate structure as soon as they have their own assistant, depending on the experience and capability of that assistant. Larger teams may benefit by including specialist roles within, or in addition to, the associate roles. When you look at your team's structure, you will have to evaluate the experience, skills and attitude of your existing team members in the context of the team structure you wish to build and the services you wish to provide to your clients.

Team Duty Allocation Spreadsheet

I have developed a downloadable duty allocation spreadsheet (see Appendix and website) to help advisors, with any team size, distribute duties amongst their team, based on the basic roles of advisor, associate, assistant to associate and administrative assistant. The advisor's delegation choices will depend on the skills and experience of their team members as well as the size of their clientele and will change as the team evolves through growth and/or turnover.

One Team Member
An advisor with only one team member would decide which duties their one assistant could handle with the remaining duties assigned to the advisor.

Two Team Members
An advisor with two team members would have the following combinations available to them:

1) One admin assistant could do some of assistant to associate role duties; the other assistant could perform assistant to associate duties plus some associate duties, with the remaining duties assigned to the advisor.

2) Divide clientele between the two team members; and both team members would handle admin duties as well as assistant to the associate duties and some associate duties, with the remaining duties assigned to the advisor.

Three Team Members
An advisor with three team members would have the following combinations available to them:

1) Administrative assistant, assistant to associate, associate

2) Administrative assistant, two associates

3) All three team members doing administrative, assistant to associate and associate roles (This would only make sense if you had three team members with equal experience, skills, etc.)

As you can see in the associate structure sample duty list provided in the appendix, some duties are performed for individual clients (RRSP contribution calls, client appointment preparation, etc.) while other duties are performed for the practice as a whole (developing a website or new process). The ease at which individual client duties are assigned to particular team members proves the natural delegation advantage of the associate structure.

Evaluating Your Current Team and Team Structure
Answering the following questions will help you evaluate your team structure:

– Are you spending too much time on day-to-day organization and delegation of tasks?

– Is there backup for every member of the team (including the advisor) for vacations, etc.?

- Are team members happy with their current roles? Do they feel limited?

- Are your team members exposed to all aspects of your practice? Should they be exposed to more?

- Can your team members see a career path within your team?

- Do your team members want to learn more and advance within your team?

- Do you have team members who are capable and willing to take on the added responsibility of an associate?

- Can you and every member of your team easily remember most of the client's circumstances, objectives and account details immediately upon answering the phone?

- Do clients have relationships with members of your team? If not, would you like them to?

- Are you comfortable sharing your client relationships with members of your team?

- Does your team have the expertise needed for the service you wish to provide your clients? If not, then should you train one or all team members, add a specialist to your team or outsource to a specialist?

I believe modifying the structure of your team could solve many of the issues that might be raised by your answers to the above questions.

———

I can't tell you how much the associate structure helped my business in dollars and cents because market volatility and other factors affect revenue too much. I can tell you beyond a doubt that I knew my clients were better served and that a client's need or request was less likely to fall through the cracks. I can also tell you that, after I adopted the associate structure, my time and my team's time was better spent and that I could relax more when I was in and away from the office.

Team Compensation

Compensation will always be a very important part of the relationship between the advisor and their team members. Perceived unfair compensation can be the elephant in the room that prevents comfortable everyday interaction. Team members need to understand how much they will be paid, when they will be paid and what they can do to increase their pay. The structure of the compensation should reflect the advisor's overall priorities of the practice and be consistent with what is expected from team members.

It is quite possible that the advisor's firm will not be willing to pay the salaries of all of the team members an advisor wishes to employ. The ambitious advisor can probably expect to pay all of the bonuses I refer to below in addition to some team members' salaries. I considered these costs to be part of growing my business and serving my clients well. I think that paying a significant portion of the team compensation costs from the revenue of my practice gave me the control necessary to allow me to design and implement a unique approach to compensating my team members. I developed a "Team Payroll Sensitivity Analysis" spreadsheet to estimate the costs and an "Advisor Actual Team Compensation Costs" spreadsheet to facilitate the implementation of this unique and flexible compensation structure. These spreadsheets are described near the end of this section and will be made available to advisors on my website.

Objectives of My Team's Unique Compensation Structure

Overall, I sought to inspire individual team members to work hard toward the common goals of the practice and have them always feel fairly compensated for their individual effort and contributions. I think a compensation structure should motivate the individual team member to always "do the right thing" for the client and the team, thereby also benefiting the advisor and the firm.

I believe that my team's compensation package accomplished the following:

- encouraged team members to feel and act like professionals
- rewarded a strong work ethic
- inspired team members to work past regular stated working hours
- rewarded extra effort quickly and fairly
- provided some consistency so team members could plan their lifestyle spending
- recognized team members for their knowledge and abilities as well as their effort
- encouraged all team members to work with each other to the benefit of all of our clients
- showed each member that they personally benefited from the team's overall success
- motivated each member to train and help other team members
- encouraged each member to back up and help other team members
- ensured that team members knew they would not suffer personally if they took time from their own duties to help, train or supervise others on the team

Bonus Components

To accomplish the above, I decided to pay team members a combination of two types of monthly bonuses over and above base salaries. The impact of these bonuses on their total pay varied with their role and contribution.

Personal Effort Bonus
This monthly bonus was loosely based on the number of hours the team member worked in excess of the regular work week, as well as

feedback from more senior team members relating to that team member's productivity. The extra hours were voluntary and encouraged. I told them that we would always have more work for them if they wished to work extra hours to increase their pay. This bonus provided an immediate financial reward for a strong work ethic whereas a lack of compensation for working extra hours might stifle a team member's enthusiasm. I saw this approach unleash many administrative assistants' ambition as they would volunteer to expand their responsibilities, knowing that they could expand their hours to fulfill those responsibilities. That attitude was a strong indication of a good long-term fit with our team. I asked each member to document their own hours on a shared spreadsheet that was visible to all team members so that I could remember how much they were working when the time came to determine their monthly personal effort bonus. This honour system regarding the reporting of hours showed a respect and trust for team members that was rarely betrayed.

Practice Revenue Bonus
Each team member received a different percentage of my practice's revenue based on my judgment regarding their contribution to the practice's total revenue. The bonus was NOT based on specific clients' revenue or revenue from specific products. This approach to bonuses aligned each team member's financial incentives with that of the advisor and the rest of the team. Everyone felt the impact of a change in the practice's revenue. This team-oriented incentive meant that team members would all benefit by backing each other up and helping when a particular assistant or associate was overloaded with client requests, answering phones, etc. This teamwork provided clients with more accessibility and quicker service. I remember many instances when one associate was working with me on a project; other team members would field their calls and take care of their duties, so they could focus on the project knowing that their assigned clients were still being taken care of.   I think this approach resulted in a happier team and exceptional client service. Clients felt comfortable and familiar with

several members of the team. This familiarity helped when a team member left, especially when my most senior associate left within two years of my retirement. When I began to give bonuses to assistants in the early stages of my career, advisor compensation was relatively simple. However, now that compensation grids are more complicated, I think many advisors may way wish to base this bonus on the advisor's payout (income before taxes). My "Team Payroll Sensitivity Analysis" and "Advisor Actual Team Compensation Costs" templates allow you to choose between basing the percentage bonus on practice revenue and basing the bonus on advisor pay.

Special Bonus

Special circumstances may arise when you feel the need to provide a bonus to a team member in addition to the personal effort and practice revenue bonus. For example, I would give a special bonus to a team member who brought in a new client through their own personal contacts.

Compensation Component Combinations for Different Team Member Roles

It is difficult to decide how much to pay each individual. Your manager or other colleagues might be able to give you ranges of total pay for people in similar roles. The overall compensation for each team member needs to be competitive with local compensation for similar roles. I have heard that people will consider leaving their current job for a 5% raise in pay. You also need to make sure you are compliant with any legal and firm requirements regarding paying for your staff's overtime.

All my team members would receive a base salary. The combination and calculation of the bonus components for each team member varied with their role, level of experience and contribution. I have described the bonus calculation structure I used for each role below.

Administrative Assistant

The new admin assistant's first raise in salary would usually come from acquiring their securities licence. The personal effort bonus would begin immediately, and the practice revenue bonus would likely start after the first year's work (or earlier, depending on performance). I reviewed their bonus structure regularly at fiscal year end and sometimes mid-year. I consulted with the rest of my team regarding the admin assistant's performance to determine the appropriate percentage for their practice revenue bonus for the upcoming year. My administrative assistant total bonuses ranged from 5% to 15% of their total pay for the last 10 years of my practice.

Assistant to the Associate

As the team member gained experience, responsibility and productivity, I would increase their monthly practice revenue bonus percentage. Eventually, the team member and I would recognize that the personal effort bonus was not appropriate for them anymore. The team member would see themselves as a professional and preferred a bonus based entirely on the practice's revenue. I would then raise their practice revenue bonus to match their personal effort bonus from the previous year. I reviewed their bonus structure regularly at fiscal year end and consulted with my associates regarding the assistant to the associate's practice revenue bonus percentage. My assistant to the associate team members' bonuses ranged from 20% to 45% of their total pay for the last 10 years of my practice.

Associate

Associates did not receive a personal effort bonus. Their practice revenue bonus percentage reflected their level of experience as well as the size and complexity of the group of clients they were assigned. The revenue bonus for associates was the biggest component of their overall compensation. I strongly believe that both the advisor and the associate should believe the ongoing compensation reflects the associate's current contribution to the practice. Their bonuses ranged from 50% to 75% of their total pay for the last 10 years of my practice.

I did not under-compensate associates with the promise that they would be rewarded with the opportunity to take over the practice. I think any such compromise in pay should be part of a formal written agreement/contract regarding the transition/group referral of clients, including a commitment of the advisor to the associate. However, I treated the purchase price of the group referral of my clients upon my retirement as a separate transaction, based on the value of those referrals at the time of my retirement. In my mind, the associates' everyday interactions with clients, the team and the advisor will show the advisor if the associate is capable of taking over the clientele. I have described in detail what an advisor should look for in a successor in the *Transitioning Clients and the Retirement Exit Decision* book's "Transitioning Your Clientele to Your Successor" (Part Two). The associate increases their likelihood of a successful transition of the clientele by providing good service and building strong relationships with the clients. In a nutshell the relationship between the advisor and associate should be a continuous win-win relationship where both the advisor and the associate always believe the current compensation is fair.

When a member of the team left, I would usually give some team members more responsibility and an immediate practice revenue bonus raise, especially when a more experienced member of the team left as everyone would be moving up a notch in responsibility.

Determining Specific Bonuses and Estimating Advisor's Total Costs

As we all know, swings in revenue will occur in most advisors' practices thanks to the wonderful world of financial markets. You need to feel confident that you can sustain your lifestyle and maintain your team's compensation during nasty markets. Obviously, you need to understand how much the total compensation of your team will be before you can promise to pay specific bonuses to each team member. The more your team grows, the more difficult it becomes to estimate your total costs, especially if some bonuses are based on unreliable revenues like the "Practice Revenue Bonus" I describe above. Even fee-based revenues can vary dramatically with stock markets. There may also be other additional related costs for each employee, such as benefits and technology. In addition to the cost issues, it was also very important to me that each members' total pay reflected their responsibilities and my judgment of their personal contribution relative to each other. I developed the "Team Payroll Sensitivity Analysis" spreadsheet to help me determine specific bonuses and to estimate how different annual revenue scenarios would affect the pay of each team member and myself, the advisor. I have modified the spreadsheet further to provide a workable template for most advisors. I have described this template in the following section.

Team Payroll Sensitivity Analysis Spreadsheet
With the help of a team member, I created a "Team Payroll Sensitivity Analysis" to be completed at the beginning of each fiscal year. It is also useful mid-year when considering adding another team member or when changing multiple team member bonuses because someone leaves the team. The analysis helped me assess my ability to sustain the team's compensation structure through bad markets by estimating my pay after all team payroll costs and non-team deductions. I am proud to say that I never downsized my team to cut costs, and I never cut revenue bonus percentages even when revenues were falling because of bad markets. In fact, I continued to raise the revenue percentages to reflect the team member's personal growth. This meant that my personal income suffered even more during bad times, but it was worth it to me to give the team a sense of income and job security when we were all dealing with the stress of down markets with our clients. The sample and template are downloadable from my website. The various tabs of the "Team Payroll Sensitivity Analysis" spreadsheet provide the following:

Instructions Tab

Provides very detailed instructions for inputting:

1) Last year's revenue and advisor's pay

2) Next year's practice revenue scenarios

3) Last year's actual team compensation and advisor's related costs

4) Next year's team compensation and advisor's related costs

5) Other non-team deductions affecting advisor pay

Input Tab

1) Summarizes "Last Year's Actual Team Compensation and Advisor's Related Costs" and "Next Year's Team Compensation and Advisor's Related Costs"

2) Allows the advisor to assess the bonuses in relation to the previous year and in relation to the individuals' roles and contributions to the team

3) Calculates last year's advisor grid payout percentage and pay after paying the team in "Last Year's Revenue and Advisor's Pay" (Note that a pull-down menu allows you to choose between "Expected Revenue $" and "Expected Advisor Payout $" as the basis for the percentage bonus.)

4) Requires inputting a variety of percentage changes to practice revenue/advisor payout to produce different scenarios and then input the related advisor grid payout percentage

5) Allows the use of multiple advisor revenue codes (i.e., extra code for a group referral)

Summary Tab

1) Easy comparison of the next year's expected compensation under different practice revenue/advisor pay scenarios for each team member, including the percentage and dollar change from the last year's actual pay

2) Easy comparison of the advisor's next year's expected costs and pay under different practice revenue/advisor pay scenarios,

including the percentage and dollar change from the last year's actual pay

Practice Revenue/Advisor Pay Scenario Tabs

Each pay scenario has a separate tab which shows the following information:

1) "Next Year's Team Member Pay" broken down by compensation components as well as their total dollar change and total percentage change over the previous year

2) "Team Members' Pay Change from Previous Year" dollar amount broken down by compensation components

3) "Next Year's Advisor Team Cost" broken down by cost categories and team members

4) "Advisor's Team Cost Change from Previous Year" broken down by cost categories and team members

Advisor Team Name
Team Payroll Sensitivity Analysis
Fiscal Year 2017-2018

Summary of the Next Year's Expected Compensation Under Different Revenue Scenarios Compared to Previous Year Before Tax

	Scenario 1 0%			Scenario 2 +20%			Scenario 3 -20%		
Revenue Change %									
Last Year's Total Revenue	$ 3,000,000			$ 3,000,000			$ 3,000,000		
Projected Revenue	$ 3,000,000			$ 3,600,000			$ 2,400,000		
Projected Advisor Payout	$ 1,400,000			$ 1,680,000			$ 1,120,000		

	Member Total Compensation			Member Total Compensation			Member Total Compensation		
	Expected	$ Change	% Change	Expected	$ Change	% Change	Expected	$ Change	% Change
Sally Smart	$ 166,500	$ 7,000	4.4%	$ 190,500	$ 31,000	19.4%	$ 142,500	$ (17,000)	-10.7%
Bob Bright	$ 132,000	$ 6,000	4.8%	$ 150,000	$ 24,000	19.0%	$ 114,000	$ (12,000)	-9.5%
Hanna Helpful	$ 77,000	$ 4,000	5.5%	$ 84,200	$ 11,200	15.3%	$ 69,800	$ (3,200)	-4.4%
Larry Leaver	$ 62,000	$ 3,000	5.1%	$ 65,600	$ 6,600	11.2%	$ 58,400	$ (600)	-1.0%
Luke Skywalker	$ 42,000	$ -	0.0%	$ 42,000	$ -	0.0%	$ 42,000	$ -	0.0%
Total Team Member Pay	$ 479,500	$ 20,000	4.4%	$ 532,300	$ 72,800	15.8%	$ 426,700	$ (32,800)	-7.1%

	Advisor Pay			Advisor Pay			Advisor Pay		
Advisor Pay Before Pay Team	$ 1,400,000	$ -	0.0%	$ 1,680,000	$ 280,000	20.0%	$ 1,120,000	$ (280,000)	-20.0%
Total Advisor Cost	$ (386,000)	$ 18,500	5.0%	$ (438,800)	$ 71,300	19.4%	$ (333,200)	$ (34,300)	-9.3%
Advisor Pay After Pay Team	$ 1,014,000		-1.8%	$ 1,241,200		20.2%	$ 786,800		-23.8%
Other Non-Team Deductions (Flat $)	$ (3,600)			$ (3,600)			$ (3,600)		
Other Non-Team Deductions (Rev %code 1)	$ (18,000)			$ (21,600)			$ (14,400)		
Other Non-Team Deductions (Rev %code 2)	$ (300,000)			$ (360,000)			$ (240,000)		
Expected Advisor Pay Before Taxes	$ 692,400			$ 856,000			$ 528,800		

Presenting New Revenue Bonus Percentages to Team Members
After I made my final decision regarding the bonus percentages, I would review the payroll analysis separately with each team member when I told them about their raise. I used the "Team Payroll Sensitivity Analysis" summary and scenario tabs to show the components of their compensation and how potential swings in practice revenue would affect their personal pay.

I liked full transparency of team member pay amongst all team members so that all team members could see what the others in the team were earning and could see how the bonuses were calculated. I also liked them to see what I was earning and my total team compensation expenses. I think this kind of transparency helps build strong honest relationships amongst all team members, including the team leader (the advisor). I am told that some members of my team were inspired by the potential to earn the higher incomes of the more senior team members who started in similar roles. Others were reassured by the obvious fairness of their bonus in relation to other team members. Without transparency, your team members would likely discuss their pay amongst themselves without giving you the chance to explain your reasoning. Transparency prevents future misunderstandings, and everyone is usually more comfortable knowing where they stand.

> *"No question: pay is one of people's favorite things to gripe and gossip about. But that's actually a great reason to be more transparent about it. Being open allows you to explain to people why others are being paid as they are. Having a good rationale for the discrepancy reinforces that you're a performance culture."*
>
> —Patty McCord
> *Powerful: Building a Culture of*
> *Freedom and Responsibility*
> *Chapter Seven: "Pay People What They're Worth to You"*

However, you will need to understand your firm's privacy policies, which may limit how much of one employee's information can be shared with another. In any case, you should ask for each employee's consent to share their information with the rest of the team. The relevant rows and columns can be easily hidden on the Team Payroll Sensitivity Analysis spreadsheet, and a spreadsheet password can be added to provide the required privacy.

Advisor Actual Team Compensation Costs Spreadsheet
With the help of a team member, I created an "Advisor Actual Team Compensation Costs" spreadsheet. The spreadsheet includes a "Total Actual Advisor Cost By Month" table and a detailed breakdown of cost components. It also includes a "Team Member Time Sheet and Monthly Compensation Calculation" for each team member and two potential bonus sheets to submit to a firm's payroll administrator. The sample and template are downloadable from my website.

— — —

Of course, it is not all about money, people need to feel respected and appreciated on an everyday basis not just when the pay cheque arrives. There are many other ways to motivate and inspire the team.

Sample Five Member Team
Advisor Actual Team Compensation Costs
Summary of Advisor's Monthly Team Compensation Costs
Fiscal Year End Date

Practice Revenue

November 2018	$ 80,000
December 2018	$ 100,000
January 2019	$ 540,000
February 2019	$ 120,000
March 2019	$ 90,000
April 2019	$ 580,000

Total Actual Advisor Cost By Month (cost component breakdown below)

	Team Total for Month	Sally Smart	Bob Bright	Hanna Helpful	Luke Skywalker	Nick Newman	Larry Leaver
November 2018	$ 32,002	$ 3,700	$ 2,400	$ 5,968	$ 9,357	$ -	$ 10,577
December 2018	$ 32,772	$ 4,000	$ 3,000	$ 6,238	$ 9,167	$ -	$ 10,367
January 2019	$ 74,772	$ 21,600	$ 16,200	$ 11,508	$ 9,517	$ -	$ 15,947
February 2019	$ 35,282	$ 4,920	$ 4,220	$ 6,868	$ 9,857	$ 9,417	$ -
March 2019	$ 31,482	$ 3,690	$ 2,790	$ 6,278	$ 9,397	$ 9,327	$ -
April 2019	$ 74,352	$ 23,780	$ 17,980	$ 12,698	$ 10,727	$ 9,167	$ -
YTD Total Cost to Advisor	**$ 280,660**	**$ 61,690**	**$ 46,590**	**$ 49,560**	**$ 58,020**	**$ 27,910**	**$ 36,890**

Cost Component Breakdown

Practice Revenue/Advisor Payout % Bonus (100% paid by advisor)

	Team Total for Month	Sally Smart	Bob Bright	Hanna Helpful	Luke Skywalker	Nick Newman	Larry Leaver
November 2018	$ 7,520	$ 3,200	$ 2,400	$ 960	$ -	$ -	$ 960
December 2018	$ 9,400	$ 4,000	$ 3,000	$ 1,200	$ -	$ -	$ 1,200
January 2019	$ 50,760	$ 21,600	$ 16,200	$ 6,480	$ -	$ -	$ 6,480
February 2019	$ 10,440	$ 4,920	$ 3,720	$ 1,560	$ 240	$ 500	$ -
March 2019	$ 7,830	$ 3,690	$ 2,790	$ 1,170	$ 180	$ 410	$ -
April 2019	$ 50,460	$ 23,780	$ 17,980	$ 7,540	$ 1,160	$ 250	$ -
YTD Revenue % Bonus	$ 136,410	$ 61,190	$ 46,090	$ 18,910	$ 1,580	$ 1,160	$ 8,640

Non-Revenue Bonus (100% paid by advisor)

	Team Total for Month	Sally Smart	Bob Bright	Hanna Helpful	Luke Skywalker	Nick Newman	Larry Leaver
November 2018	$ 1,690	$ 500	$ -	$ 300	$ 440	$ -	$ 450
December 2018	$ 580	$ -	$ -	$ 330	$ 250	$ -	$ -
January 2019	$ 1,220	$ -	$ -	$ 320	$ 600	$ -	$ 300
February 2019	$ 2,300	$ -	$ 500	$ 600	$ 700	$ 500	$ -
March 2019	$ 1,110	$ -	$ -	$ 400	$ 300	$ 410	$ -
April 2019	$ 1,350	$ -	$ -	$ 450	$ 650	$ 250	$ -
YTD Non-Revenue Bonus	$ 8,250	$ 500	$ 500	$ 2,400	$ 2,940	$ 1,160	$ 750

Total Bonus (paid by advisor)

	Team Total for Month	Sally Smart	Bob Bright	Hanna Helpful	Luke Skywalker	Nick Newman	Larry Leaver
November 2018	$ 9,210	$ 3,700	$ 2,400	$ 1,260	$ 440	$ -	$ 1,410
December 2018	$ 9,980	$ 4,000	$ 3,000	$ 1,530	$ 250	$ -	$ 1,200
January 2019	$ 51,980	$ 21,600	$ 16,200	$ 6,800	$ 600	$ -	$ 6,780
February 2019	$ 12,740	$ 4,920	$ 4,220	$ 2,160	$ 940	$ 500	$ -
March 2019	$ 8,940	$ 3,690	$ 2,790	$ 1,570	$ 480	$ 410	$ -
April 2019	$ 51,810	$ 23,780	$ 17,980	$ 7,990	$ 1,810	$ 250	$ -
YTD Total Bonus	$ 144,660	$ 61,690	$ 46,590	$ 21,310	$ 4,520	$ 1,160	$ 9,390

	Team Total for Month	Sally Smart	Bob Bright	Hanna Helpful	Luke Skywalker	Nick Newman	Larry Leaver
Advisors % Share		0%	0%	50%	100%	100%	100%
Base Pay (received by team member)							
November 2018	$ 16,833	$ 3,833	$ 3,500	$ 3,417	$ 2,917	$ -	$ 3,167
December 2018	$ 16,833	$ 3,833	$ 3,500	$ 3,417	$ 2,917	$ -	$ 3,167
January 2019	$ 16,833	$ 3,833	$ 3,500	$ 3,417	$ 2,917	$ 2,917	$ 3,167
February 2019	$ 16,583	$ 3,833	$ 3,500	$ 3,417	$ 2,917	$ 2,917	$ -
March 2019	$ 16,583	$ 3,833	$ 3,500	$ 3,417	$ 2,917	$ 2,917	$ -
April 2019	$ 16,583	$ 3,833	$ 3,500	$ 3,417	$ 2,917	$ 2,917	$ -
YTD Base Pay	$ 100,250	$ 23,000	$ 21,000	$ 20,500	$ 17,500	$ 8,750	$ 9,500
Benefits including employer share of Canada Pension Plan (CPP) and Employment Insurance (EI)							
November 2018	$ 22,500	$ 4,500	$ 4,500	$ 4,500	$ 4,500	$ -	$ 4,500
December 2018	$ 22,500	$ 4,500	$ 4,500	$ 4,500	$ 4,500	$ -	$ 4,500
January 2019	$ 22,500	$ 4,500	$ 4,500	$ 4,500	$ 4,500	$ -	$ 4,500
February 2019	$ 22,500	$ 4,500	$ 4,500	$ 4,500	$ 4,500	$ 4,500	$ -
March 2019	$ 22,500	$ 4,500	$ 4,500	$ 4,500	$ 4,500	$ 4,500	$ -
April 2019	$ 22,500	$ 4,500	$ 4,500	$ 4,500	$ 4,500	$ 4,500	$ -
YTD Benefits	$ 135,000	$ 27,000	$ 27,000	$ 27,000	$ 27,000	$ 13,500	$ 13,500
Quotes/Tech							
November 2018	$ 7,500	$ 1,500	$ 1,500	$ 1,500	$ 1,500	$ -	$ 1,500
December 2018	$ 7,500	$ 1,500	$ 1,500	$ 1,500	$ 1,500	$ -	$ 1,500
January 2019	$ 7,500	$ 1,500	$ 1,500	$ 1,500	$ 1,500	$ -	$ 1,500
February 2019	$ 7,500	$ 1,500	$ 1,500	$ 1,500	$ 1,500	$ 1,500	$ -
March 2019	$ 7,500	$ 1,500	$ 1,500	$ 1,500	$ 1,500	$ 1,500	$ -
April 2019	$ 7,500	$ 1,500	$ 1,500	$ 1,500	$ 1,500	$ 1,500	$ -
YTD Quotes/Tech	$ 45,000	$ 9,000	$ 9,000	$ 9,000	$ 9,000	$ 4,500	$ 4,500

Motivating/Inspiring the Team

"Motivation is the external/extrinsic or internal/ intrinsic reason we take action on a particular task. External motivation often shows up in the form of a reward, such as money, fame, grades, or praise. Internal motivation is driven by our innate psychological needs: competence, autonomy, and psychological relatedness. Basically, this means we like to feel we are good at something, are making a difference and enjoy being self-directed and connected to others."
—www.forbes.com/sites/forbescoachescouncil/ 2017/08/09/you-cant-motivate-your-team-but-you-can-inspire-them

I agree wholeheartedly with the definition provided above by Forbes. I would add that motivation can also stimulate the energy and desire to enhance or perfect activities.

I strongly believe that an advisor should consider motivational factors when developing or reviewing most components of a financial advice practice as an extension of the "win-win" approach. Everyone benefits from a motivated team member: clients, advisors, firms, teams and obviously the actual team member. Incorporating motivating factors in the thought process for assigning duties and developing processes for your practice will result in energized, happier and more productive team members who are also more likely to stay with the team long-term. My personal experience, common sense and comments from former team members have led me to believe that an individual team member's motivation will increase with a combination of motivating factors that appeal to them as an individual. I have collected many of these motivating factors into the seven categories below followed by further clarification and ways to provide these motivating factors to a financial advisor's team.

Motivating Factor Groups

1) Personal Benefits: The team member is confident they will personally benefit from their efforts.

2) Feeling Productive: The team member can see tangible results from their work.

3) Personal Recognition: The team member can see that clients, team members, the advisor and/or firm management appreciate and respect their efforts and abilities.

4) Feeling Appreciated: The team member should feel appreciated on an everyday basis not just when the pay cheque arrives.

5) Making a Difference: The team member can see that their efforts are benefiting others (clients, team members, the advisor and/or firm management).

6) Being Part of Something Bigger: The team member can see they are an integral part of a team.

7) Empowerment: The individual needs to know it is within their personal power to do what is necessary to increase personal benefits, be productive, achieve personal recognition and make a difference.

As we go through the many examples of motivating factors, it is important to recognize that each team member is unique and will therefore value each factor differently due to their DNA, personality, character and previous life experiences as well as their personal circumstances. The value each team member places on the various factors will likely evolve with the stages of their career and personal life. For example, compensation usually becomes more important as time progresses because as individuals age, their personal, financial responsibilities increase, and the team member rightfully expects to be paid for their increased productivity, knowledge and skills. The importance of each factor and how a team leader can provide those factors will vary with each individual.

Personal Benefits

The advisor who aspires to motivate their team members to work hard and do their best must ensure that their team members benefit personally from their efforts and that the team members recognize and value those benefits. I expect there are many potential personal benefits that may be unique to particular practices and/or team members; however, I think many of those personal benefits will come in the following forms:

Compensation

A team member needs to see and believe in the potential for increased immediate and future monetary compensation based on their efforts. This handbook's section on "Team Compensation" provides details of the bonus structure I used to provide both short- and long-term motivation.

Knowledge and Skill Development

Most new hires told us they were motivated to take a job on our team because of the opportunity to gain knowledge and develop skills to become productive and successful in the financial industry. To ensure that employees maintained this motivation, we provided training as described previously in this handbook, with an emphasis on industry courses, technology and software, hands-on training and learning from the experience of others.

The following quotes provide evidence that this education did indeed motivate team members:

> *"Chris never shied away from exploring new technologies and implementing procedures and practices in order to help us in our duties and to attain our goals. In addition, she pushed both her team and the firm to provide us the training to do so. Above all, she prized education and self-*

improvement, and as such, our suggestions and opinions were always valued within the team. This helped to boost morale."

—former associate

"Learning and using the newest technology/computer programs made coming to work more fun."

—former associate

I often pushed team members to stretch their Excel skills by asking them to create a presentation/template beyond their current skill set. I am told they were motivated by my confidence in them and by their understanding and acknowledgment that the end result was worth achieving.

Gaining Experience and Exposure to Various Areas of the Financial Industry

In the early stages of a team member's career, gaining experience and exposure to various areas of the financial industry is usually very important to them as they look to uncover their interests and their personal strengths. It is important that the team member is gradually exposed to and involved with as many aspects of the financial industry as is reasonable within the context of their abilities. I tried to make sure a team member received some new duties and responsibilities when their learning curve appeared to stagnate as they became proficient in their current duties. My team members were exposed to many areas of the financial industry—actual money managers, securities research, securities trading, fintech, banking, trusts, financial planning, life insurance and other advisors as well as branch and firm management including advisor support groups. I believe the structure of the team and an advisor's willingness to include and involve team members in all aspects of the business can provide the experience and exposure team members are looking for to motivate them through the various stages of their career.

Opportunities to Advance Own Career Within the Team
Regardless of the size of the team, the advisor needs to show each member how their duties and responsibilities with the team can be expected to progress as they gain knowledge, skills and experience. I provided a clear and achievable career path for my team members through the associate team structure described earlier in this book.

> *"I have always wanted to be an advisor. I looked forward to continually learn, expand my ability and experiences. I was always striving to prepare myself for the next step, more challenging tasks and greater responsibility. For me, the timing of departures within the team allowed for opportunity for me to continue to accomplish my career goals."*
>
> —an associate
> (who eventually took over part of my practice)

Of course, anything done to help a team member advance within the team is also preparing them for a career in the financial industry outside the team.

Opportunities to Advance Own Career Within Financial Industry
I was willing to help team members if they decided to pursue a career outside my group, hopefully after they had worked for me for at least two years. Occasionally, the individual knew their desired career path before joining the team, and we agreed during the hiring process that they would work for me for a period of at least two years. After two years, I would help them take the next step on their desired career path.

> *"You asked me what I wanted, and I said that I wanted to be an advisor. You said that if I committed to you for two years, you would help support me getting into the firm's rookie training program, which is exactly what happened…. Your manager told me that I would learn more about being an advisor from*

*two years on your team than I could in my first 10
years as an advisor with my own practice. This was
good advice."*

—former team member
(who has now been an advisor for over 20 years)

You can point to the success of previous team members to motivate
potential new hires and current team members, show your ability to
open doors for them and establish your commitment to a win-win
relationship. Knowing that I had helped a well-known mutual fund
manager move from being my assistant to the next step in his career
proved to my team members that I cared about their success even if
they had to leave my team to achieve it.

*"Thank you for giving me my start in the financial
services industry. I've told countless people how once I
told you it was time for me to move on, you actually
helped me find a job in research. I'll never forget what
you did for me."*

—Paul Musson
Lead portfolio manager Ivy Foreign mutual fund

Feeling Productive

A team member will usually be motivated by feelings of
accomplishment when they see their finished work product. These
visible results of their productivity can be as simple as a finished
report, a client review presentation, a financial plan or a list of
activities completed during a day. Breaking large projects into
smaller parts with identifiable points of completion will also provide
an energy boosting productive feeling and help maintain motivation
throughout the project.

A good contact management system can help team members feel
the satisfaction of completing each individual activity, similar to
crossing an item off a written to-do list. It should show them when
all of the tasks assigned for the day have been dealt with and allow

them to quantify their daily accomplishments (for example, completed 20 activities) by providing a detailed list of the activities they completed that day. A contact management system's ready-made to-do list for the next day, week, month, etc. should give the team member confidence that they can continue to be productive.

Advisors who use macros, templates, checklists and calculators in their processes will help staff be and feel more productive. Allowing them to contribute to the development of those processes will likely add to their productivity and motivation. I intend to include examples of such processes in a future handbook about processes and presentations.

An advisor should work to perfect their processes by identifying and preventing obstacles that would prevent or slow a team member's completion of a task. It is important to give the team member the job and then get out of their way. I would try to be available as much as possible for reviews and to address their questions quickly so they could get back to getting the job done. I worked hard to avoid being the bottleneck in the productive process. The sooner they could complete a task the more productive and motivated they felt. I have found that motivation is greatest when the team member feels ownership of a project, and they are empowered to carry it out from start to finish.

Personal Recognition

I think it is fair to say that most people are motivated and likely energized by receiving personal recognition from others. An advisor should ensure that each team member receives the appropriate amount of recognition and appreciation while understanding that each individual might value each form of recognition and appreciation differently. This recognition may come in a variety of ways: from clients, the advisor, fellow team members and the firm. I have listed some examples below.

Positive Feedback on Day-To-Day Work
Acknowledgment/recognition of specific good work and extra effort should happen in the moment it occurs. When a team member has stayed late to serve a client, suggested a great idea, etc., make sure you say thank you or tell them that you appreciate their commitment and contributions. If you can do so in front of other team members or people ... all the better! Be sure to pass on good comments from clients and to give credit where credit is due regarding contributions to the team. These contributions might include ideas involving the improvement of processes, presentations, and templates, and insights into managers.

> *"Receiving positive feedback from clients directly, or through my Investment Advisor, really pushed me to perform better and accomplish more. Important for client to say it, important for advisor to pass it on."*
> —former associate

A Promotion or Increased Responsibilities
An advisor's promotion of the team member and/or delegation of increased responsibility recognizes the team member's good past performance and shows the advisor's confidence in the team member's ability to do more.

Respect
An advisor's continuous requests for, and willingness to listen to, the team member's opinions, feedback, ideas, etc. shows personal recognition through respect.

Transparent Bonus Compensation Structure
A compensation bonus structure that is personalized to reflect an individual's effort and productivity is good personal recognition; however, transparency of this bonus structure within the team members is even better. My approach to team compensation has been explained in great detail in this handbook's "Team Compensation" section.

Titles

The team member's title should denote status as well as indicate a level of experience, expertise and responsibilities to fellow employees and clients.

> *"Clients respond to the "associate" title, more professional, knowledge that advisor is extending more trust to the team member."*
>
> —former associate

Personnel Evaluations

The use of personnel evaluations should allow for honest, individualized recognition and positive constructive comments as well as advice for improvement. Properly done, personnel evaluations are the opportunity to recognize good employees and be a source of motivation. Unfortunately, some policies regarding these evaluations have the opposite effect, so I have included further comments in the "Preventing Demotivation" section of this book.

Feeling Appreciated

For most people, feeling appreciated inspires loyalty and a willingness to work harder. People should feel appreciated on an everyday basis not just when the pay cheque arrives. I have listed several of my attempts to show appreciation to my team. I expect that none were strong motivators by themselves but as a whole resulted in the team members feeling appreciated and experiencing more on-the-job enjoyment.

Seasonal

Every Christmas, I would give small gifts (probably a gift certificate) to each team member with a Christmas card containing a personalized note expressing my appreciation for them, their skill set and their contribution. In late November/early December, I would also host a team dinner at my home or a local restaurant for everyone and their spouses or significant others. During the summer

I would often arrange a team get-together in the form of a Major League Baseball game, dinner or barbecue—usually including team members' spouses or significant others. The gift and dinners might serve the dual purpose of helping the employees' spouse see that I appreciated the extra effort and hours that were sometimes required.

Celebrations

I would often buy a cake or have a pizza lunch for the team to celebrate a team member's birthday or the passing of an industry exam by someone on the team. As well as showing the team that I cared about them, it also showed the importance I placed on continuing education and their long-term success. A further benefit was the opportunity for team members and myself to spend some casual time together.

Length of Service Recognition

I gave a special recognition present to members of my team after 10 years with me (usually a gift certificate to a store that reflected their interests). I would consult with the employee to get them something that they wanted and would truly appreciate. Most importantly, the present was something that probably had nothing to do with the business. One of my long-standing team members has told me that he still remembers what I gave him and thinks of me every time he sees his gift!

Departing Team Members

When you lose a valuable team member to a better opportunity for them or a life-changing situation, it is important to show them appreciation for a job well done, regardless of how disappointed you may be personally. This appreciation can be shown in many ways ranging from a small gift to a special lunch or team dinner. It is the right thing to do and sends a good message to the rest of the team. For example, I gave a "going away" team dinner for the associate that left shortly before I retired. It was the right thing to do for many reasons. Most importantly, he deserved it. He had worked hard for our clients and the team for approximately 18 years. He had taken excellent care of the clients and had trained numerous team members. He had served as a valuable sounding board for me for many years. I was very surprised and disappointed by his departure but appreciated his professionalism during his tenure on my team as well as his approach to leaving. I believe it also sent a positive message to the remaining team members.

Making a Difference
One of the biggest motivators for a human being is seeing another person benefit from their hard work. It is important that a team member understands how their efforts make a difference in the lives of clients, fellow team members, the advisor and/or firm management.

I expect that every advisor's practice is intended to make a positive difference in the lives of clients. This is often articulated in the advisor's "value proposition" or "commitment to clients". A team member who understands and agrees with how the advisor intends to help clients will be motivated when their advisor shows them how and why each activity they perform is expected to help. It does not hurt to remind team members how important our job is: that clients are trusting us with their financial well-being and that our advice will affect clients' ability to take care of their family, their retirement lifestyle and their ability to give to charity.

I believe the motivation is strongest when there is a relationship with the individual you are helping. The more a team member knows the real person benefiting from their efforts, the more they will care, and the more motivated they will be "to go the extra mile" and provide a top level of service. Introducing clients to the team members that do the work for them and encouraging direct contact, will usually motivate those team members. During client meetings the associate would see the use of all of the schedules, agendas, financial plans, etc. that they had spent time putting together and how the client benefited from the information.

> *"Clients have always been my primary source of motivation. Building and growing relationships with clients and their families was and continues to be a key driver for me."*
>
> —former associate

Team members may also feel they are making a difference in the lives of fellow team members by providing training and helping them be more efficient and effective.

Being Part of Something Bigger

Many of my team members have mentioned that they liked being part of our team. Obviously, working in an atmosphere of mutual respect with people that the team member likes and trusts creates a bond where team members are motivated to help the team succeed. We fostered this team spirit and sense of belonging in many ways.

Include Members of the Team on Major Decisions

The inclusion of team members in major decisions, such as the development of processes, selection of investment securities and money managers as well as the hiring of new team members, shows the team members that they are respected and that their intelligence, skill set and contributions are valued.

> *"Our suggestions and opinions were always valued within the team. This helped to boost morale, and truly made us feel as though we were a part of something important."*
>
> —former associate

Promote Team Attitude

Team members were expected to back each other up for vacations and help each other out when workloads became unbalanced. They were encouraged to ask each other for help and training.

Compensation Based on Total Team Revenue
As you will see in this book's section on "Team Compensation", my team members received a bonus based on the team's total revenue.

> *"Giving each member of the team a percentage of revenue made everyone feel like they were part of something."*
>
> —former team member

Share Your Successes with Your Team
Make sure your team members know that you realize that their individual efforts made your successes possible. These successes include a good meeting with a client or prospect, deposits of new assets from existing or new clients, the creation or modification of a helpful process, the identification of an attractive investment product, reaching production or asset gathering goals as well as the firm's recognition of the advisor's achievements.

Include All Team Members in Marketing Materials
I included all team members on my website, my brochures, my Christmas card team picture and on my business card. I listed assistants on the back of my business card until my team grew to four team members. I then listed all team members on the inside of a folding business card.

Recognize Team Members as Unique Individuals Within the Group

> *"People are happier in groups that provide optimal distinctiveness, giving a sense of both inclusion and uniqueness. These are the groups in which we take the most pride and feel the most cohesive and valued."*
>
> — Adam M. Grant
> *Give and Take: Why Helping Others Drives Our Success*
> *Page 233*

I think it is important for team leaders to remember this and resist the desire to force team members to conform completely.

Many of the acts of appreciation discussed previously will also contribute to a team member's sense of being a part of something bigger. Team lunches and dinners, etc. involved participation of the entire group leading to friendly casual interaction. These team gatherings in a social setting were meant to build camaraderie and the feeling of belonging to a team.

Empowerment

Empowerment is ensuring team members are enabled to work effectively, efficiently, productively and independently with minimal supervision or interference from the advisor, fellow team members or firm management. Empowerment is necessary to maximize the contributions of the above motivating factor groups to an individual's motivation. The individual needs to know they are within their personal power and control to do what is necessary to increase their personal benefits, be productive, receive personal recognition and make a difference. Helplessness is a huge demotivator. I have listed below some tools and opportunities that work together to help empower team members.

Training
Good training empowers team members to perform their duties and complete their daily tasks independently.

Increase Independence
As team members grew in knowledge and capability, I expanded their duties to include independently making and carrying out decisions without close supervision.

"I felt truly empowered when you trusted me to make many decisions independently relating to clients' portfolios. For example, rolling bond maturities, generating funds for RRIF payments, small client cash requests, etc."

—former associate

Involve Team Members in Decisions That Affect Them Directly

Involving team members in decisions, like hiring team members they will work with and selecting the securities and managers that they will personally be recommending to clients, will give them a feeling of personal control and positively affect their performance.

Templates, Macros and Calculators

These tools allow even the least experienced team member to work productively and independently without constant supervision or intervention. Customized templates and calculators containing instructions and self-checking features make it easier for team members to do their job and catch their own mistakes.

Up-To-Date Technology

I always wanted to work with new technologies myself and soon realized that if the technology helped me be more effective it would likely do the same for my team members. I often supplied my team with new technology well before my firm, even if it meant paying for it myself. Some examples of this include up-to-date software, hands-free phones, remote access capability, printers, scanners as well as online meeting and video conferencing.

Contact Management System

The disciplined use of a good contact management system by all team members facilitates empowerment by providing a ready-made to-do list every day for each team member. The to-do list is usually linked to related notes regarding previous conversations and activities involving themselves and other team members. This easy form of communication reduces the need to interrupt other team members and fosters independence for even the newest team member.

Remote Access

I set up remote access capabilities for senior members of my team to allow them to occasionally work from home. I think it compelled them to be more engaged and encouraged thinking about the business when not in the office.

> *"Remote access is great, especially since I moved to a house out of downtown. I often check my e-mail, etc. from my home computer on weekends. I would not do that without remote access."*
>
> —former team member

It was also useful for a team member with family responsibilities.

> *"I was relieved that remote access allowed me to do much of my job while I was at home caring for a sick child."*
>
> —former associate

Preventing Demotivation

Demotivation is worse than a lack of motivation. Demotivators stifle initiative, deflate confidence, dampen enthusiasm, drain energy and take the fun out of work. The resulting frustration and reduced productivity ultimately lead to poor client service and staff turnover. I have listed some demotivators I noticed throughout my career. I expect every practice is different and that each advisor will need to be on the lookout for these examples and many others.

Examples of Demotivators

– monotonous repetitive tasks

– long delays between steps in a process and completion of the task

- bottlenecks and roadblocks to productivity that prevent the quick effective completion of tasks
- inefficient technology and equipment
- lack of ability to build on previous work/accomplishments
- changing or contradictions in "long-term" priorities
- feeling underutilized
- feeling overqualified
- not enough work to do
- feeling that the work is meaningless
- useless meetings
- unwillingness of advisor or firm to explain the "why" behind activities and policies
- lack of job stability
- fear of making a mistake or not meeting expectations
- unrealistic expectations (hours and productivity)
- unclear instructions
- uncomfortable physical environment

Identify Demotivators Through Observation and Open Lines of Communication

Identifying demotivators affecting an advisor's practice usually provides opportunities to discover and fix inefficiencies and increases the utilization of team talents. It will also improve the advisor's relationship with team members by showing a willingness to support them and make their jobs better. An advisor needs to observe their team to understand how everyone is spending most of their time, constantly looking for ways to modify, minimize and even eliminate processes that demotivate team members. When I noticed a team member spending a long time on a recurring task, I reviewed the details of the process with the team member to discover roadblocks and bottlenecks as well as find opportunities to streamline the process and remove the monotonous repetitiveness of the task. Regardless of how good the advisor's processes are, there is probably room for improvement.

A good employee may be reluctant to tell you about demotivators because they want to be seen as a team player and don't want to be seen as a complainer. As a result, they may be willing to suffer through demotivating poor processes "for the benefit of the team" or see it as "paying their dues". I like the attitude but would rather improve the process where possible. Employees should be encouraged to point out "there has to be a better way to do this", especially when faced with a repetitive, monotonous task. Advisors should remind team members that their feedback is welcome, and their suggestions will be implemented if they make the process more efficient and effective.

Minimize or Remove the Drudgery
Advisors and team members should always look for ways to automate repetitive and menial tasks. Sometimes advances in technology can be used to eliminate menial jobs (group emails instead of stuffing paper envelopes). If you find yourself or a team member making very similar notes for various clients, consider creating a macro of a standard note to be used by all members of the team. I was reluctant to accept "It is a lousy job, but someone has to do it". I intend to provide some of the templates, macros and calculators we used to minimize repetitive tasks in my future handbook about processes and presentations.

Minimize or Eliminate Roadblocks and Bottlenecks
- Advisors should make sure they are not the bottleneck for task completion by making themselves readily available for questions, approvals, etc.

- Processes should be designed to minimize process flow interruptions caused by the involvement of multiple people or departments.

- An advisor should be willing to step in to eliminate a roadblock. For example, I would sometimes step in to escalate an issue to back office supervisors.

- Advisors should provide access to the best equipment and technology available even if that means spending their own money.

Support/Back Up Team Members

If your firm or industry is doing something that demotivates team members, show your team members that you understand their plight and do your best to minimize the damage to morale. For example, a firm might require seemingly onerous amounts of new paperwork or reporting. I believe that advisors should point out these issues to management and/or the industry where appropriate. Your team members will appreciate this support even if you don't succeed in changing the policy. An advisor should work with their team to devise processes to meet the requirements while minimizing the time and effort of their team.

Poor Personnel Evaluation Policies

I know that some firms' policies declare that only a small percentage of employees can be considered "outstanding" on formal personnel evaluations. At first glance this arbitrary decision may seem logical. However, the implementation of the policy is very demotivating and frankly sends a bad message to all levels of management, employees and anyone who knows the policy, including clients. I would think every firm should be aiming for more outstanding employees instead of deciding that only a small percentage of the entire firm could possibly be outstanding. Some of these policies allow only one or two associate/assistants of a branch to be considered "outstanding". Such a policy is clearly demotivating. An advisor can limit the damage by telling the affected team member that the firm policy prevented the advisor from giving the top rating the advisor believes they deserve and by including very positive comments, where permitted in the evaluation.

Dealing with Mistakes

When a mistake occurs, an advisor's first instinct may be to focus their disappointment/anger on the employee responsible. However, it is usually better to focus on the process in an attempt to reduce or eliminate the recurrence of the mistake instead of focusing on the individual. This approach requires some discipline on the part of the advisor but will likely result in better solutions and will take the pressure off the employee. Too much direct criticism of the individual may paralyze them with the fear of making future mistakes thereby stifling their productivity.

Admit When You Are Wrong

Don't be afraid to admit when you are wrong about something. Your stubbornness will discourage your team from giving valuable input which may prevent future errors, loss of business, etc. Your stubbornness may result in the loss of your best and brightest employees. Who else would be able to see your mistakes or be smart enough to foresee problems that might be caused by a bad decision? An advisor who refuses to admit they are wrong will create an unhappy environment and unpleasant place to work. Team members will be less likely to put in extra effort for the advisor or for clients and be very unlikely to come up with and/or share ideas. Best of all, admitting when you are wrong allows you to improve your practice for the benefit of everyone.

An advisor's attention to the motivating factor groups as well as working to minimize demotivators should all go a long way towards creating an environment where highly motivated, energized team members enjoy coming to work every day.

Team Meetings

Informal Impromptu Team Meetings

I am a great believer in informal impromptu team meetings. Our team of eight or less (including myself) was small enough to gather on a moment's notice. Our meetings were called as the need arose to disseminate information quickly to the team or to make a decision affecting many clients or the overall practice. Occasionally, we had multiple team meetings in a week and sometimes there were several weeks between meetings. My office door was open unless I was in a client meeting, and my team members were comfortable coming to see me as soon as issues arose. We would call the rest of the team into my office when all could benefit by the discussion and/or their views were needed. Everyone was encouraged to contribute their observations, ask questions and make suggestions. Different perspectives were welcome. Even the newest team members would contribute occasionally. This allowed myself, the team and my practice to benefit from the combined skills, knowledge and experiences of all of the team members. The meetings usually resulted in timely, well-thought-out decisions and/or a plan to address the issue.

Team Meeting Topics

- market events (discuss client's reactions and our responses)
- discuss news and/or performance of particular securities and managers
- inclusion in meetings with a money manager visiting our office
- change of a lead portfolio manager for one of our recommended mutual funds or separately managed accounts
- choosing a new mutual fund or separately managed accounts manager

- new issues (e.g., a new preferred share offering) to discuss the pros and cons of the issue and if suitable for any of our clients
- new firm policies and how to implement them efficiently and effectively
- workload allocation amongst team members
- hiring a new person
- team member departures
- celebrating a team member's achievement

Experience with Regularly Scheduled Meetings

On the suggestion of a team member, we did try scheduling weekly team meetings about 15 years into my career. However, many meetings were canceled for lack of agenda items because no one wanted to wait for the scheduled meeting to address the issues at hand. Waiting for a regularly scheduled meeting would delay the decision and require writing down more thoughts to ensure no ideas were lost, creating more work and a roadblock for the team member attempting to complete an activity. As a result, team members requested the continuation of impromptu team meetings. After a year or so, I determined that no one wanted to prepare for or attend the weekly meetings and that reserving a time slot in the calendar for the team meeting was reducing flexibility for scheduling client appointments. The regular meeting felt too bureaucratic and unproductive. I did not want to cause the "useless meeting" demotivator, so I called an impromptu team meeting, and we decided to abandon the scheduled weekly meeting idea.

Perhaps a larger team or a team that does not communicate with each other as much on an ongoing basis would find regularly scheduled meetings more beneficial than we did. However, I would discourage delaying the discussion of everyday issues. Such delays could affect team productivity, slow down client service and adversely affect the motivation of your team members.

Relationships with Team Members

An advisor's relationships with each of their team members is more important than the advisor's relationship with most individual clients simply because the team members work for and, in most cases, communicate with many clients every day. An advisor naturally works hard to empathize with each individual client. I think advisors should work even harder to empathize with their team members to understand what is important to them and to learn what is needed to help them serve clients well. Empathizing with team members should be easier for those who evolved from the assistant/associate role into the advisor role. They should be able to remember the work, the experiences and how they felt when they were in those positions; although, they may have to remind themselves that team members may have different ambitions and priorities than they did at the same point in their careers. All advisors should recognize that team members are unlikely to care about their practice as much as the advisor.

I think it is very important to have a 1:1 bond with each team member regardless of how new they are to the team and how little experience they might have. Even the least experienced and lowest paid team member should feel comfortable coming to the advisor's door even though they may be intimidated by the advisor's position. It is an advisor's job as team leader to put them at ease and be as approachable as possible. The price for unapproachability can be very high. Team members will be reluctant to share their good ideas or point out weaknesses in the practice. They might avoid showing the advisor a problem until it has grown far larger than necessary.

1:1 Lunches

I used to take each team member out to lunch separately every few months in an effort to build stronger, direct relationships. We would discuss what was going on in their lives, their aspirations and their personal interests (hobbies, sports teams, music, movies, etc.). The lunches would help a new hire see me as human and may have made it easier for them to come to me with issues and questions in the future. One of my long-time team members told me that others would return from a 1:1 lunch with me saying that they saw a different, less intense me with outside interests. It would also give them a chance to voice any concerns out of earshot of other team members. These conversations helped me put myself in the team member's shoes and understand their sources of stress from both inside and outside our office. I would learn what motivated them and discover demotivators that may have been affecting their performance. I am also told that these 1:1 lunches made the assistant/associate feel appreciated.

Show Interest in Team Member's Career

An advisor should show an interest in their team member's career goals and help them to reach them wherever possible. An advisor can help a team member determine which of the many industry courses they should take first, based on their long-term goals. An advisor must accept the fact that not all good employees belong on their team long term but remember that an advisor with the reputation of treating team members well will attract stronger candidates to replace those who leave.

Patience with Brief Periods of Underperformance

An advisor will benefit from having the patience to let a good employee work through a period of underperformance caused by personal distractions. One might say that personal lives should not interfere with one's work, but reality says otherwise. Such patience is far easier to justify when the employee has given you good effort and performance in the past. Losing a good long-term employee because of a short-term personal problem seems foolish. We all know how hard it is to find a good team member. An advisor's patience and understanding will likely instill loyalty and camaraderie in the whole team, not just the affected team member. I can think of several occasions where I was patient with employees dealing with demanding family situations. I know the individuals recognized and appreciated my understanding. Advisors are not immune to personal distractions and periodic underperformance. The goodwill stored from patience with team members may help them forgive an advisor for some of their own imperfections.

———

Strong relationships with team members are helpful when seeking to provide many of the motivational factors previously mentioned in this handbook. If an advisor's relationship with team members is honest, fair and open, they will be more productive and will likely stay with your team longer. Work will be more fun and comfortable for all.

Team Member Turnover

Turnover happens! And often it happens when you least expect it.

My worst case of unexpected turnover happened approximately eight years into my career. I came back from a vacation and my manager told me that we should go for a walk. We were good friends, so I did not think much of it. At the time I had a team of two assistants that I was very happy with and whom I thought were happy. My manager told me that while I was away, my longest serving assistant told her that he had decided to move into a different area of the financial industry. I remember saying something like "Well that is disappointing because I think he has a lot of potential, and I will miss him and the good job he is doing. The silver lining is that my newer assistant is ready and willing to take over his duties and will really enjoy the challenge". Then the other shoe dropped.... She told me that the other assistant was also leaving for a totally different job in the financial industry. I went from a team of two good assistants to a team of zero. I stressed out to the point of getting a migraine, and I actually interviewed candidates with the lights off; although, we were not in complete darkness because of light from the window. The silver lining—I hired Paul Musson who is still a friend today and so are the two assistants that left. Stuff happens!

Even though I am told my team had relatively low turnover, approximately 50% of our new hires did not stay past 1.5 years. I reviewed my last 20 years of team members and discovered that team members staying past 1.5 years were usually with me for five or more years unless personal issues necessitated a change. I think an advisor has done well if a team member stays longer than five years, especially if the advisor is hiring inexperienced candidates as I did. I remember thinking when I approached two years without losing a single team member (out of a team of six), that someone would probably leave soon ... and they did! As my practice was often the new hire's first exposure to the financial advice industry, many left when they or we realized they did not belong on my team or in the industry. Two members of my team left in the same year several times during my career.

The larger your team, the more likely and more often you can expect to lose team members. However, the larger the team, the easier it is to absorb the turnover. Turnover is not necessarily a bad thing, even if you are losing a good employee. The loss of an employee almost always leads to opportunities for the remaining team members. As team leader it is up to the advisor to make the best of it for their clients and the remaining team members.

If you have a strong, productive team, you will likely have done a good job of motivating your team and minimizing team member turnover. In this section I will review many reasons why turnover happens. I hope to help advisors make peace with the fact that a great deal of turnover is beyond their control while also encouraging them to step back and learn what they can from the situation for the benefit of their practice and the remaining team members. I will identify some opportunities that turnover provides and give you some ideas to help you make the most of those opportunities.

There are essentially two types of departures from a team:

1) Non-performing team members
2) Valued team members

Non-performing Team Members

Regardless of how good your hiring process, you can expect that some of your team members will fail to live up to expectations. Usually, my team or I would realize the new hire was not going to work out within six months. We often chose to err on the side of patience before making a final decision on parting ways, especially if the new hire had a good attitude. I always relied on the senior members of my team and branch administrators/compliance officers as well as my branch manager for input to help me evaluate team members and make decisions regarding the retaining or firing of underperforming team members. These team and branch members sometimes experienced different behaviour as many team members would be on their best behaviour around the boss/advisor.

Understand the Underperformance Before Giving Up

It is important to try to understand the reasons behind a team member's underperformance before you give up on them. Perhaps the reasons are temporary and reversible. As mentioned earlier, the advisor's door should always be open to all members of the team, and the advisor should be working to maintain a relationship with each team member, including underperforming team members. Conversations, including the team member's explanations for underperformance, will likely reveal a lot about the team member's attitude. Do they explain gaps in their knowledge and skills? Do they have or seek a plan of action to improve? Do they blame everyone else for their shortcomings? A team member's attitude was always the most important factor to me. A good attitude can compensate for knowledge and skills. Knowledge and skills CANNOT compensate for a bad attitude. This is true largely because a person with a good attitude will work to gain the missing knowledge and skills. I recommend reviewing the training and motivational sections of this book in relation to the underperformer's experience on your team to ensure that you and your team have done all that you should do to help them succeed. You should also consider the points raised in "Patience with Brief Periods of Underperformance" in the "Relationships with Team Members" section of this handbook.

Are Advisor Expectations Reasonable?

An advisor clearly has a long-term, vested interest in their practice, similar to a small business owner. Although my suggestions in the motivation, team structure and team compensation sections are designed to help the team member feel like part of the business, it is unfair and unrealistic to expect the same level of commitment as the advisor. When an advisor is still building their business, they are likely working hard and long hours and may, consciously or unconsciously, expect their team members to work as hard as they do. This unrealistic expectation will likely lead to advisor disappointment and reluctance to show appreciation for the team members' effort and accomplishments. This lack of appreciation will likely cause tension and demotivate team members.

Reasons to Fire Someone or Feel Relieved When They Quit

- lack of respect for and adherence to industry regulations

- lack of respect and sensitivity to other people

- incapable of performing their duties with speed and accuracy after a reasonable period on the job

- careless attitude

- lack of attention to detail

- numerous errors repeated several times

- lack of sense of urgency (let down clients and other team members)

- unreliable attendance

- inability to pass industry licencing exams

- lack of commitment to career and client service (leaves early when everyone else is working late)

- disagreement with approach to investing and service model

- lack of rapport with fellow team members

- unreasonable pay expectations/demands

- attitude/too good for the job

- arrogance: One new assistant told an experienced assistant that she would be showing her how to do things within a few weeks. Another member thought he could take a day to play golf because he felt like it. (We found out when he did not show up for work that day.) Another member thought he was superior to branch administrators with 10+ years' experience.

Costs of Keeping A Non-performing Team Member

An advisor is often reluctant to fire an underperforming team member because they don't want to lose what little is being accomplished while they go through the hiring process to find a replacement and, of course firing someone is, to say the least, unpleasant for all involved. However, the longer the advisor keeps the non-performing team member, the longer everyone suffers. The advisor owes it to the non-performer, the other team members and the clients to end the suffering. The non-performer continues to struggle in a job with no future surrounded by team members who are frustrated with their lack of performance. Their underperformance is likely dragging down the performance, productivity and morale of other team members who are forced to correct errors and waste time following up on the non-performer's unfinished tasks. Errors and omissions can hurt financially as the advisor must reimburse the affected client for damages caused by costly errors. The advisor loses credibility with clients when an underperforming team member's errors and poor attitude become apparent to clients. I remember one assistant's lack of sense of urgency resulted in numerous cheque issuing delays. How could anyone not see how important receiving a cheque is to a client? One client waited until after I had fired an assistant to tell me she was glad the assistant was gone because the assistant's insensitivity had brought her to tears more than once. This taught me that clients would not always tell me when an assistant was treating them poorly. It is important that an advisor and team members keep their eyes and ears open.

All of the above costs should convince you that delaying the firing of a non-performing team member hurts everyone (clients, team members and you). It even hurts the non-performing employees as their bad habits are being formed and practiced for as long as you allow them to continue. The sooner they leave your team, the sooner they will be able to search for a more suitable job that they can flourish in. It is always difficult to know just how patient you should be. I believe that the better the attitude of the employee, the more time you should give them. A hardworking, respectful employee, who is good with clients, deserves your patience. However, once you have determined that they are not capable and likely not going to become capable, you owe it to them and the rest of the team to let them go. A bad attitude is no fun for anyone to be around. A non-performing team member with a bad attitude needs to be removed from your group as soon as possible to minimize the damage to morale and client relationships.

Firing Non-performers

Be honest, fair and gentle when you fire people. Try to avoid humiliating them, offer some positive advice and help them with their next career move when it is reasonable to do so. We would often give the non-performing team member the opportunity to look for a new job while still employed by me, especially if they had a good attitude. Many years ago, I let an assistant go after he struggled in the admin roll. We liked him and could see that he was intelligent and had excellent people skills. I told him that he was probably well suited to be an advisor even though he was not well suited to be an admin assistant. Years later he contacted me after having opened his own financial planning practice. He told me that he had found my comments very encouraging and thanked me for the experience.

Ask Departing Team Member Why It Did Not Work Out

The advisor and the non-performing team member might both benefit from an honest discussion regarding why the job did not work out for them. This discussion may not be comfortable; however, it will give the employee a chance to express their views. They may tell the advisor they felt unfairly treated, poorly trained, that too much was expected of them, etc. Although it is never fun to hear these things, the lessons learned may prevent the loss of present and future team members. It is important for an advisor to ask themselves if they failed the non-performing team member or made a mistake hiring the person. The advisor should consider reviewing the hiring and training sections of this handbook in the context of the departing member's comments and experience to see if there was anything more that should have been done or if something was missed in the hiring process.

Don't Let Turnover Affect Your Long-Term Vision

You may have suffered through a bad experience with a non-performing or borderline team member. You may feel that they were not worth the money you paid them or the time spent training. It is important to realize that the reasons for needing the team member have not changed. Just because that particular hire did not work out, does not mean you should shrink your team. Hopefully, you will have learned from the experience. Don't let a short-term disappointment in one individual affect your long-term vision for your practice.

Valued Team Members

I expect that most experienced advisors have lost at least one valued team member who believed their future was better served elsewhere. My relationships with team members were very important to me, especially after several years of working closely together. As a result, especially early in my career, I would feel personally disappointed and sometimes hurt if they left me for another opportunity. I was most surprised and disappointed when I lost a high performing, senior team member (which occurred four times in my last 20 years). I needed to remind myself that it was a business relationship and that each individual must manage their own career according to what they believe is best for them. The biggest surprise of all happened when my longest serving associate left to move to Asia after 18 years on my team and less than two years before my retirement. Very few assistants remain with an advisor for an entire career. There may have been nothing an advisor should have done, or not done, to keep a person longer, but it should be given serious thought.

Quality Team Members Are Not Always a Long-Term Fit

There are many reasons why a high performing team member may choose to leave your team. I have listed many such reasons below grouped by compatibility issues, personal reasons and attractive opportunities elsewhere.

Compatibility Issues

- disagrees with investment strategy

- disagrees with service model (For example: use of financial plans)

- disagrees with team structure

- wants to specialize in a different part of the industry

- realizes they are not interested in the financial advice industry (likely within first two years)

- wants to work with a different clientele (level of wealth or sophistication)

- uncomfortable communicating directly with clients

> *"I preferred to work behind the scenes supporting the advisor instead of facing/communicating directly with clients."*
> —former valued team member who went on to be the head branch administrator of a very large branch

- not comfortable with and/or not capable of the associate role

> *"I liked client relationships, but I found the responsibility of a client's life savings to be 'scary'."*
> —former valued employee

- uncomfortable with size or structure of the firm (bank owned vs independent)

Personal Reasons

- joins a future spouse living in another city (three of my assistants did so)

- wants to live elsewhere (one of my team members left for British Columbia, another moved to Asia)
- desires a work location closer to home
- stay home with children

Attractive Opportunities Elsewhere
- learning opportunities (another advisor with different investment approach or service model)
- experience different career in the financial industry (banker, research analyst, etc.)
- significant raise in pay
- wants to be an advisor with own practice without waiting for current advisor to retire
- pursue additional formal education (MBA, etc.)

Sometimes the team member has been offered a great opportunity well beyond or very different from what you could offer them. If you think they are making a mistake, I think you owe it to them to tell them what you think, but beyond that you should just wish them well. If you are lucky, and you desire it, you will maintain good relationships with many of those who leave your team.

> *"I thought I would be with your team for my whole career but then the unusual opportunity to become a CFO for a small company came along."*
>
> —former team member
> (who remains a client of my successor today)

Ask Departing Valued Team Member Their Reasons for Leaving
After you recover from the shock of the news, you should try to probe for and really understand their reasons for leaving. Was their compensation inadequate? Did they think their opportunities were limited? There may have been absolutely nothing that you could have done better, but you might discover demotivators in your

practice or realize that you are not doing enough to motivate your team. When a valued team member chooses to leave your team, you should consider reviewing the entire motivation section of this handbook in the context of the departing member's comments and experience.

Opportunities Arising from Team Member Turnover

Looking back, even the departures of my most valued employees usually had a "silver lining". Good things can come out of losing even the most valuable team member.

> *"Every time I started to feel like it might be time to look, someone on the team quit, and I got a promotion with new responsibilities and a raise."*
> —an associate on my successors' team

Opportunity to Promote Remaining Team Members

Generally, the greater the responsibilities of the departing team member, the more painful the loss for the advisor. However, it also means greater opportunity for more members of your team. If an associate left my team, every other team member likely benefited with greater responsibility and an increased bonus. If an assistant to an associate left, the admin assistant and probably another assistant would benefit the most.

Opportunity to Raise Pay for Team Members and Advisor

If an experienced member of the team left, I would hire an inexperienced person at a lower salary and much lower bonus. This gave me more money to raise the revenue-based bonus to the remaining team members to go along with their increased responsibilities. It also usually gave me a temporary raise with the flexibility to add to other team member bonuses in the future. The distribution of the departing team member's bonus was fair compensation as we would all have to spend more time training and adjusting for the loss of the experienced team member.

Bonding of Remaining Team Members

Remaining team members have the opportunity to pull together and prove that they are at least as strong as they were before the other left. I usually noticed a sense of pride in the remaining team members, especially when a senior team member left. They were determined that the clients and I did not feel the loss. It is the advisor's opportunity to show increased confidence in the team as a whole and as individuals.

Opportunity to Re-evaluate Team Structure and Allocation of Duties

As described in the "Estate Planning Assistant" portion in the "Specialist Structure" section of this handbook, the first time the most senior member of my team chose to leave was a valuable learning opportunity prompting an immediate change to my team structure. I did not move another member of the team into his role that was dedicated to life insurance/estate planning upon his leaving, and I basically abandoned the specialist structure. The flexibility of an associate team structure allows for modifications within the structure through the reallocation of duties easily facilitated by the "Team Member Duty List" shown in the appendix and available through my website.

Consider Revising Your Hiring Process

On my team, the most recent hire (the admin assistant) was the team member most likely to leave. They were likely leaving because of their lack of interest in the financial advice industry, or we were letting them go because of underperformance. Usually this meant they were not pulling their weight, and the rest of the team was suffering for it. I would likely give a small raise to the team member who had most recently performed the admin assistant duties as they would be most involved in the hiring process and then training the new hire. We would all be even more motivated to hire the right person the next time, especially if the departing admin assistant was a poor performer. When you lose a team member within the first year or so, you may benefit by reviewing your hiring process. You may wish to add some questions to your hiring interviews in hopes of detecting incompatibilities and minimizing unrealistic expectations of the next hire. It may be helpful to review the "Hiring New Team Members" section of this handbook.

Minimizing Turnover Damage

Almost everything mentioned in this series of books is intended to help advisors train, motivate and nurture a strong team which should in turn minimize turnover. In addition, you should continuously give and remind team members about opportunities within your group. You can hope a team member will give you a chance to discuss pros and cons before they decide to move on; however, it is usually a well-kept secret until you are presented with the news as a "done deal". The advisor's next goal should be to minimize the damage caused by the turnover.

Departure of an Associate Who Has Client Relationships

When an associate who has relationships with clients leaves, the advisor should call the affected clients along with the replacement associate to inform them that the current associate is leaving and introduce them to the team member who will be assuming the day-to-day relationship with them. Nobody likes to discover, without warning, that the person they are used to dealing with on a daily basis has disappeared. If the departing associate is leaving the business or country, they should be included on the call if possible and will likely receive many thanks, accolades and good wishes from the clients. If the departing associate is staying in the financial advice business, they should likely leave immediately with no further contact with clients.

Minimize Gaps in Experience Caused by Turnover

I found it best that a new team member performed the admin assistant role for at least one complete year. This way they would experience, at least once, all seasonal activities, such as tax reporting, tax-loss selling, retirement plan contributions and rollovers as well as beginning and end of the year contributions to registered education and savings plans. However, sometimes unexpected turnover can result in the promotion of an admin assistant before they have completed a full year in the role. I recommend involving the promoted assistant in the completion of the seasonal duties they have missed, likely sharing the related duties with the new hire.

Contact Management System

A good contact management system will help the remaining team members pick up where the departing team member left off, assuming that they made good notes and left notifications for future actions. The items on to-do lists should be easily reassigned.

Part on Good Terms

Parting on good terms is best. Although it may be very difficult at the time, I think an advisor should try hard to remain on good terms with both valued and non-performing, departing team members. Think about the message you want to send to the remaining team members. Many of my former team members and their families still have accounts with my team today. You never know what the future holds.

I once lost an associate because he wanted to be a stay-at-home dad. I was very disappointed as he was extremely productive, and many clients had told me how much they appreciated him. However, we parted on very good terms. I told him that when he was ready to come back to work, I would welcome the opportunity to see if I had a place for him. Several years later when his boys were in school full-time, he suggested working part-time for me. Of course, I leapt at the opportunity, and he has been working part-time for me ever since. In fact, Mike has worked with me from the beginning in the writing of this book and on the modification of many of the templates and spreadsheets mentioned in this book.

Of course, an advisor will also minimize the damage by recognizing and capitalizing on some of the previously mentioned "Opportunities Arising from Team Member Turnover".

— — —

Most of the reasons for a team member's departure have nothing to do with the advisor or their practice. In many cases, there is nothing that can be done to prevent it. The decision to part ways is not necessarily a failure on the part of anyone but simply the end of a mutually beneficial relationship.

Key Takeaways

A good team will allow an advisor to build a bigger and better practice. I believe my practice grew to five times the size it would have been had I not built a team. I also believe it would have grown faster and larger if I had added to my team sooner and if I had adopted the associate structure sooner.

Every advisor's practice is different, and every advisor's clients are different; therefore, each advisor's delegation decisions will likely be different. However, I encourage all advisors to push themselves to delegate as much as possible. Remember, "If someone else can do it, someone else should do it.", and "If you don't enjoy doing it, someone else should do it". The appendix provides a list of potential duties for each of the team member roles and an overview of how the team's time is spent. My website provides a customizable template to help with the distribution of these duties.

An advisor should always be asking themselves and their team members questions to determine if their team is big enough to provide the service and growth they wish to achieve. A team member should be added when the practice can benefit from the increased delegation and can afford the expense.

When hiring we looked for humility, curiosity, common sense, people skills and determination along with a strong work ethic as well as a desire to help people. An applicant with the relevant knowledge, education and skills would get an interview, but the best attitude got the job.

To build a successful team, the advisor must be willing to sacrifice time in the short term to train team members. Training your team is an excellent investment that will pay off in the long term. The best training can be done naturally within the normal course of business (getting the job done for your clients while the training is taking place). Good training leads to engaged, happy and productive team members who serve clients well. As the team grows, the benefits compound as the team members train and learn from each other.

The right team structure will provide a clear definition of roles resulting in less confusion and greater peace of mind for clients, team members and the advisor. A good team structure will result in systematic delegation of most tasks giving team members more independence and autonomy. It will provide quality backup for the advisor and team members in their absence. The right team structure will maximize the productivity of every member of the team and provide career paths with opportunities for learning and advancement.

Team members need to understand how much they will be paid, when they will be paid and what they can do to increase their pay. Each team member's bonus should relate to the team member's personal effort as well as the overall practice revenue. The structure of the compensation should reflect the advisor's overall priorities of the practice and be consistent with what is expected from team members.

An advisor's attention to team member motivational factors as well as working to minimize demotivators will go a long way towards creating an environment where highly motivated, energized team members enjoy coming to work every day.

I think it is very important for the advisor to have a 1:1 relationship with each team member regardless of how new they are to the team and how little experience they might have. Even the least experienced and lowest paid team member should feel comfortable coming to the advisor's door.

When team member turnover happens, remember to look for the "silver lining". Good things can come out of losing even the most valuable team member if you look for the resulting opportunities.

Customized templates, checklists, calculators and macros will facilitate training for team members and help to maximize team productivity.

A good contact management system shared by your team is needed to facilitate the delegation and supervision of duties in addition to providing access to notes regarding conversations with and services provided to clients by the advisor or other team members.

Conclusion

More for Everyone

A good team will benefit the advisor, their clients, the individual team members and the firm. My willingness to build and nurture a team allowed me to expand my service to existing clients and pursue more clients resulting in a bigger and happier clientele, which naturally produced more revenue to be shared by myself, my team members and my firm in keeping with the win-win concept.

Clients

"You and your team have done a great job for us over these many years. We are enjoying our retirement in part because of the guidance and service that you and your team have provided."

—long standing client of myself and my successor

"Chris always seemed to gather people around that seemed to know what they were doing, they were young and learning the business, but they always struck me as being competent. But more than that, they seem to recognize the interests of the client, and they look after the client just as well as Chris does. In other words, they reflected her."

—Dennis Dack (client of 30 years)
Retired Director of Strategic Policy
Advisor to the Chairman of the Board
Ontario Hydro

Team Members

> *"A well-structured team with defined roles, emphasizing streamlined processes, templates and an emphasis on continuous improvement, meant that the team grew together.... By recognizing our accomplishments, working with us through our problems and compensating us fairly, she instilled a strong work ethic we could then pass on to others."*
>
> —former associate

> *"I would not be where I am today without you. Funny thing is ... I didn't realize the impact you made until I'd left the team."*
>
> —former associate

The Firm

Firms benefit when strong teams make their advisors more productive and provide better service to clients. Better served clients will be more inclined to send referrals and act as ambassadors for both the advisor and the firm. A strong well-managed team will also provide the firm with loyal well-trained employees including future advisors. A team can provide the relationship continuity necessary to maximize the retention of clients upon the retirement of an advisor. The best successor may come from the team and the supporting team members can work with any successor advisor thereby minimizing the client's need to develop new relationships.

Advisor

The advisor will have more time to do what matters to them: grow their business and/or enjoy more personal time. I believe most of the ideas and tools discussed in this book can be universally applied to most financial advisor practices even though every practice is unique. The *Business Models for Financial Advisors* handbook in this series provides many examples of how team members can help an advisor serve clients through investment strategy and selection, financial planning, marketing and client communications.

The final benefit of having a good team will come with the advisor's retirement. The best successor will often come from the advisor's own team. In many cases team members will continue with the successor advisor even if the successor advisor is not a team member. Both scenarios provide clients with continuity and a greater likelihood of a smooth transition.

For many advisors their team is their most important resource. It certainly was for me! Cultivating a happy, motivated and productive team will go a long way to ensuring a successful practice with satisfied clients thereby providing a financial advisor with peace of mind.

Afterword: COVID-19

There is nothing like a serious crisis to bring a team together (or break it apart)

As I began the process of self-publishing the first three handbooks in this series, the world and the financial advice industry were suddenly facing the COVID-19 world pandemic health crisis. In addition to healthcare workers and people infected by the virus, the crisis dramatically affected the everyday lives and financial circumstances of a huge number of people in the world as countries closed their borders, schools, stores and restaurants, maintaining only essential services. Arts, sporting and social events around the world were canceled, and large populations were confined to their homes. Individuals, including advisors, team members and clients, faced major challenges relating to childcare and eldercare. Economic activity ground to a halt; unemployment soared to historic levels; stock markets plummeted, and many businesses struggled to survive government mandated closures. The businesses that survived had to adapt to a new world of "social distancing".

While living through this crisis, I reviewed the topics discussed in this handbook with the effects of the crisis in mind. The benefits of team building and good team management remain. Advisor's teams who had already implemented many of the tools mentioned in this book were able to continue to run their practice with minimal interruption from the COVID-19 crisis.

The biggest impact of COVID-19 on the financial advice industry appears to be the forced use of technology for all stakeholders (advisors, team members, firms and clients). Technology is being applied to replicate office capabilities within advisor and team member homes. Some advisors and firms who had been slow to adopt new forms of technology were forced to expand their methods of communicating, delegating, supervising and training to compensate for social distancing. Others who had already embraced many of the new technologies are learning even more ways to improve team communication and efficiencies. The following technology tools have been available but underutilized by many teams and firms until forced into use by the social distancing required by COVID-19.

1) Remote access

2) Contact management systems

3) Virtual meetings (video and/or document sharing)

4) Online chats (instant messaging)

Remote access

During the COVID-19 crisis, access to firm data, trading systems, contact management systems, etc. from home became mandatory for most, if not all, advisors and team members. Up to date remote access technology ensures that you are ready to work from home to deal effectively with unforeseen events, such as pandemics, terrorist events and natural disasters as well as personal or family illnesses. Many advisors experiencing remote access for the first time will realize how helpful and convenient home access can be during normal times.

Contact management systems

Advisors' use of remote access during the COVID-19 crisis has highlighted the importance of a good contact management system. A good system allows tasks to be delegated and assigned without the need for verbal communication while providing access to notes from all team members. This becomes absolutely necessary when the team cannot be together physically and casual interaction is not as easy. Depending on a contact management system should result in the added benefit of more concise and accurate instructions and note taking.

Virtual Meetings (video and/or document sharing)

The benefits of virtual meetings (video and document/screen sharing) became evident to many advisors for the first time as they were forced to collaborate with and supervise team members while working in different locations because of COVID-19.

Virtual meeting screen sharing allows multiple team members to view and edit a document on each other's computer screen. This ability is extremely helpful while collaborating on the design and content as well as the review of documents and presentations. It is especially effective in reducing the back and forth for minor revisions. I expect that many advisors will continue with this efficient approach to collaboration and reviews after everyone returns to the office. Advisors and team members will also likely discover that screen sharing is an excellent training tool for job shadowing and demonstrating the use of software, macros, templates, etc.

Team members will still be able to participate in client meetings. They can join and leave virtual meetings in progress with less disruption than they could during a physical meeting. Team members may find it easier to take notes on their computer during a virtual meeting.

Online Chats (instant messaging)

Casual online chat benefits became evident to many advisors as they attempted to replace the readily available verbal communication of an office environment. Instant messaging allows team members to replicate some of the casual conversation that helps create a healthy work environment. Online chats facilitate the asking of quick questions without having to connect via the phone and prevents tying up a line. Online chats should be encouraged to maintain open lines of communication amongst the advisor and team members, similar to an open-door policy. Those teams using online chats for the first time during COVID-19 might continue its use for casual interaction when teams return to the office to prevent having to leave one's desk or "talk across the office".

All four of the tools mentioned above can empower team members by giving them more independence while maintaining the ability to ask for assistance and clarification as well as encouraging communication within the team. Being forced to learn how to work remotely with team members through contact management systems, virtual meetings and online chats should show many advisors how these tools can be used to create a more efficient practice, even when they return to a more traditional work environment.

Advisors will have to work extra hard to motivate, inspire and maintain strong relationships with team members. Technology can improve communication in some ways but can't fully replace the personal one-to-one contact that motivates and inspires a team. Team members working in isolation will be less likely to see the big picture of client service. Advisors will have to make an effort to ensure that team members continue to receive personal recognition, feel appreciated and feel that they are part of something bigger. Scheduled and spontaneous virtual face-to-face team meetings or one-to-one meetings, where everyone can see each other, may go a long way to compensate for the lost casual day-to-day interactions of an office environment and maintain team cohesiveness.

Cautionary Note

The short-term success of working from home during COVID-19 may create a temptation for firms to move more staff away from the office long term to save real estate costs and travel time. However, I believe that doing so will create many long-term weaknesses. Working from home weakens the ability of new team members to learn from senior members through hearing their conversations with clients. There will be less opportunities to share day-to-day positive and negative experiences thereby limiting the ability to build and maintain strong camaraderie amongst team members. Working from home removes the natural setting for the interaction and sharing of ideas amongst peers outside the team. New relationships with peers and mentors will likely be more difficult to develop, and firm culture and loyalty will be harder to establish. Branch managers will find it more difficult to mingle with advisors, associates and assistants without the ability to physically walk around the branch.

———

A crisis like COVID-19 can be an extremely destructive and disruptive force throughout the world. As financial advisors, it is our job to minimize the impact on our clients and to search out opportunities to serve them better. As team leaders, it is our job to minimize the impact on our team members. Doing so will result in win-win scenarios where our clients, our team and our firms will benefit.

Appendix: Team Member Duty Lists

The sample team duty lists shown below identify many of the duties I delegated in my last years of practice. The duties/tasks are listed in roughly the same order as the topics covered in my business models handbook. The associate structure sample and the specialist structure samples show the same duties distributed amongst the different team members. The team member duty list templates on my website are easily modified to fit to any structure or combination of structures, any number of team members and an infinite number of duties. A firm can facilitate their advisor's assigning of clientele relationships to their associates by providing household rankings with various metrics, such as revenue generated, assets under management, fee-based revenue, etc., similar to what an advisor needs if they are segmenting their clientele (see Business Models for Financial Advisors handbook). These rankings will help an advisor understand an associate's total overall workload and may be part of the criteria considered in the assignment process. For example, an advisor may wish to put the larger relationships with the more experienced associate.

The overview of the team monthly hours spent in the various categories of duties and tasks will help the advisor analyze the time spent in relation to the advisor's goals for their practice to determine if the time spent correlates with the intended focus of the practice.

Associate Structure Sample

The associate structure sample reflects my use of the associate team structure three years before I retired and includes an estimate of the time spent on each duty by each team member. In the interests of my successor advisor's privacy, the business attributes (# of households, revenue and assets) shown are NOT accurate portrayals of my business at that time but do reflect a reasonable distribution of duties amongst associates with differing levels of experience.

Associate Structure Sample

Duty / Task	TEAM TOTAL	Advisor	Assoc 1	Assoc 2	Junior Assoc	Asst to Assoc 1	Asst to Assoc 2	Admin Asst	Out-source
		Name	Name	Name	Name	Name	Name	Name	Name
Assigned Households	300		80	120	100				
Assigned Households Assets ($)	420,000,000		225,000,000	150,000,000	45,000,000				
Assigned Households Revenue ($)	3,000,000		1,500,000	1,125,000	375,000				
Monthly Total Hours (target 160 to 200)	1158	158	166	175	177	156	153	167	6

OVERVIEW (team monthly hours by category)

Duty / Task	TEAM TOTAL	Advisor	Assoc 1	Assoc 2	Junior Assoc	Asst to Assoc 1	Asst to Assoc 2	Admin Asst	Out-source
Marketing - Group	33	6			4		20	2	1
Marketing - Individual Prospect	10	10							
Client Contact - Group	20	3		9				3	5
Client Contact - Individual Client	474	74	118	118	75	25	25	39	
Investments - Common Stock Picking - Group	0								
Investments - Group	63	8	7	7	7	22	7	5	
Investments - Individual Client	208	20	28	28	54	39	39		
Financial Plans - Individual Client	51	12	6	6	7	10	10		
Insurance - Individual Client	16	7	3	3	3				
Tax Return and Tax Strategy Services	36		3	3	10	10	10		
Admin - Group	39	5			5	8		26	
Admin - Individual Client	175	8	1	1	11	37	37	88	
Technology	13	2			1	1		2	
Team Management	13	2				4	5	2	
Practice Analysis	7	1			1			2	

Associate Structure Sample (continued)

Duty / Task	TEAM TOTAL	Advisor Name	Assoc 1 Name	Assoc 2 Name	Junior Assoc Name	Asst to Assoc 1 Name	Asst to Assoc 2 Name	Admin Asst Name	Out-source Name
Marketing - Group									
Writing prospect communications	15	3					12		
Generate list of prospects	5	1					4		
Deliver communications to prospect list	2							2	
Marketing events	5	1					4		
Website design / maintenance	6	1			4				1
Marketing - Individual Prospect									
Pursue identified compatible sustainable prospects	10	10							
Client Contact - Group									
Christmas cards for clients - creation	6							1	5
Christmas cards for clients - distribution	1							1	
Write newsletters	4	1		3					
Write market update letters / e-mails	4	1		3					
Write money manager update letters / e-mails	4	1		3					
Write stock update letters / e-mails	0								
Write contribution reminders (RRSP, RESP, etc.)	1							1	
Client Contact - Individual Client									
Client meetings with advisor and associate	64	32	12	12	8				
Client meetings associate and assistant	8		4	4					
Preparing for appointments: agendas	24	10	1	1	2	5	5		
Preparing for appointments: reports	46	10	4	4	8	10	10		
Miscellaneous client calls / e-mails	150	10	40	40	20	10	10	20	
Proactive calls: convert to managed money	55	5	20	20	10				
Proactive calls: convert to fee-based	55	5	20	20	10				
Preparing bond call macros	5							5	

Associate Structure Sample (continued)

Duty / Task	TEAM TOTAL	Advisor Name	Assoc 1 Name	Assoc 2 Name	Junior Assoc Name	Asst to Assoc 1 Name	Asst to Assoc 2 Name	Admin Asst Name	Out-source Name
Client Contact - Individual Client (continued)									
RESP withdrawals	2							2	
RESP contributions	2							2	
RRSP contributions	15		5	5	5				
RRIF withdrawals	15		5	5	5				
TFSA contributions	15		5	5	5				
Re-orgs	3		1	1	1				
Flowers / cards / gifts for clients	5							5	
Christmas baskets for clients	5							5	
Meetings with clients' lawyer / accountant	5	2	1	1	1				
Investments - Common Stock Picking - Group									
Common stock screening (monthly +)	0								
Common stock research / report reading	0								
Updating common stock scripts	0								
Review research with advisor and team	0								
Investments - Group									
Research investment ideas	4					4			
Team meetings to discuss investment ideas	21	3	3	3	3	3	3	3	
Money manager lunches and presentations	27	5	4	4	4	4	4	2	
Money manager research	5					5			
SMA* manager performance spreadsheet (monthly)	2					2			
MF manager performance spreadsheet (monthly)	2					2			
SMA* buy / sell monthly reports	2					2			

Associate Structure Sample (continued)

Duty / Task	TEAM TOTAL	Advisor Name	Assoc 1 Name	Assoc 2 Name	Junior Assoc Name	Asst to Assoc 1 Name	Asst to Assoc 2 Name	Admin Asst Name	Out-source Name
Investments - Individual Client									
Prepare current portfolio spreadsheets	30				10	10	10		
Maturing bond/GIC calls	30		10	10	10				
Stock trade calls	0								
Prepare individualized client spreadsheets	40		5	5	10	10	10		
Preparing recommendations	30		5	5	10	5	5		
Review recommendations with advisor	48	20	8	8	4	4	4		
Implementing / checking recommendations	30				10	10	10		
Financial Plans - Individual Client									
Gather data	5				1	2	2		
Input into financial planning software	5				1	2	2		
Create plan and associated graph	15				3	6	6		
Review plan	6	2	2	2					
Present plan to client	20	10	4	4	2				
Insurance - Individual Client									
Identify insurance opportunities / needs	6	3	1	1	1				
Prepare insurance quotes and recommendations	4	1	1	1	1				
Meet clients to review insurance proposals	6	3	1	1	1				
Premium reminder calls / e-mails	0								

Associate Structure Sample (continued)

Duty / Task	TEAM TOTAL	Advisor Name	Assoc 1 Name	Assoc 2 Name	Junior Assoc Name	Asst to Assoc 1 Name	Asst to Assoc 2 Name	Admin Asst Name	Out-source Name
Tax Return and Tax Strategy Services									
Tax loss selling	2		1	1					
Minimize tax impact: mutual fund year end distribution	2		1	1					
Tax package preparation	15				5	5	5		
Client gain / loss spreadsheets for taxes	17		1	1	5	5	5		
Admin - Group									
Sort mail	5							5	
Filing	5							5	
Identify incoming cash and securities	5							5	
Review previous day transactions and revenue	10	5						5	
Mutual fund trailers reconciliation	1							1	
Review debit balances to find errors	2					2			
Review credit balances for cash to invest	2					2			
Restricted list follow-up (documents)	5							5	
Monthly managed money fees (reconciliation)	2					2			
Quarterly managed money fees (reconciliation)	2					2			
Admin - Individual Client									
Opening new accounts / verify banking info	40					10	10	20	
Updating KYCs	40					10	10	20	
Documents and signing with advisor	16	8				2	2	4	
Converting RRSPs into RRIFs	4							4	
Requests sent to / from back office	45				5	10	10	20	
Issue cheques / electronic funds transfer	10							10	
Account transfers follow-up	20					5	5	10	

Associate Structure Sample (continued)

Duty / Task	TEAM TOTAL	Advisor Name	Assoc 1 Name	Assoc 2 Name	Junior Assoc Name	Asst to Assoc 1 Name	Asst to Assoc 2 Name	Admin Asst Name	Out-source Name
Technology									
Various hardware problems / software problems	5				5				
Contact management system maintenance	1				1				
Design templates / macros	7	2			5				
Team Management									
Track team professional development (CE credits)	1							1	
Reconcile advisor pay statement (team payroll deductions)	2						2		
Payroll spreadsheet maintenance and bonus sheet	3	1					2		
Team meetings	7	1	1	1	1	1	1	1	
Practice Analysis									
Daily incoming asset tracking	2							2	
Revenue tracking by platform	1					1			
Monthly production and forecast spreadsheet update	1					1			
Update asset mix tracking spreadsheet (monthly)	1					1			
Monthly asset allocation / segmentation / mix	1					1			
Review practice analysis reports	1	1							

*SMA -Separately Managed Accounts

Specialist Structure Sample

The following sample shows a reasonable distribution of the same duties/tasks amongst the team members of a team using the specialist structure. The advisor would be expected to carry the heaviest load of client contacts, and only the advisor would have the wholistic view of each client's situation. The time spent on each task would vary with the emphasis of the advisor's practice. The advisor in this example emphasizes stock picking, financial planning and the pursuit of new clients. The template provided by my website allows an advisor to add and modify duties/ tasks and the number of team members.

Specialist Structure Sample

Duty / Task	TEAM TOTAL	Advisor	Mktg Specialist	Est Plan Specialist	Stock Specialist	Tech Specialist	Admin Specialist
		Name	Name	Name	Name	Name	Name
Monthly Total Hours (target 160 to 200 per team member)	1122	217	178	184	196	179	168
OVERVIEW (team monthly hours by category)							
Marketing - Group	62	3	55	2	2		
Marketing - Individual Prospect	15	5	10				
Client Contact - Group	49	6	35	2	6		
Client Contact - Individual Client	356	117	53	70	37	50	29
Investments - Common Stock Picking - Group	69	11	5		53		
Investments - Group	61	10	10		33	8	
Investments - Individual Client	178	27		8	58	85	
Financial Plans - Individual Client	80	15		65			
Insurance - Individual Client	22	4		18			
Tax Return and Tax Strategy Services	28	2		14	2	10	
Admin - Group	46	5					41
Admin - Individual Client	97	4	5				88
Technology	13	2				11	
Team Management	36	5	5	5	5	11	5
Practice Analysis	10	1				4	5

Specialist Structure Sample (continued)

Duty / Task	TEAM TOTAL	Advisor Name	Mktg Specialist Name	Est Plan Specialist Name	Stock Specialist Name	Tech Specialist Name	Admin Specialist Name
Marketing - Group							
Writing prospect communications	21	1	20				
Generate list of prospects	10		10				
Deliver communications to prospect list	5		5				
Marketing events	13	1	10	1	1		
Website design / maintenance	13	1	10	1	1		
Marketing - Individual Prospect							
Pursue identified compatible sustainable prospects	15	5	10				
Client Contact - Group							
Christmas cards for clients - creation	7	1	6				
Christmas cards for clients - distribution	2	1	1				
Write newsletters	15	1	10	2	2		
Write market update letters / e-mails	11	1	8		2		
Write money manager update letters / e-mails	8	1	6		1		
Write stock update letters / e-mails	5	1	3		1		
Write contribution reminders (RRSP, RESP, etc.)	1		1				
Client Contact - Individual Client							
Client meetings with advisor	60	40		10	10		
Client meetings with specialist	10			5	5		
Preparing for appointments: agendas	45	15	10	10	10		
Preparing for appointments: reports	50	5		10	5	30	
Miscellaneous client calls / e-mails	60	10	10	10	5	10	15
Proactive calls: convert to managed money	20	10	10				
Proactive calls: convert to fee-based	20	10	10				
Preparing bond call macros	10					10	

Specialist Structure Sample (continued)

Duty / Task	TEAM TOTAL	Advisor Name	Mktg Specialist Name	Est Plan Specialist Name	Stock Specialist Name	Tech Specialist Name	Admin Specialist Name
Client Contact - Individual Client (continued)							
RESP withdrawals	13	4	1	4			4
RESP contributions	11	4	1	4			2
RRSP contributions	11	4	1	4			2
RRIF withdrawals	13	4	1	4			4
TFSA contributions	11	4	1	4			2
Re-orgs	2				2		
Flowers / cards / gifts for clients	5	1	4				
Christmas baskets for clients	5	1	4				
Meetings with clients' lawyer / accountant	10	5		5			
Investments - Common Stock Picking - Group							
Common stock screening (monthly +)	3				3		
Common stock research / report reading	45	5			40		
Updating common stock scripts	6	1			5		
Review research with advisor and team	15	5	5		5		
Investments - Group							
Research investment ideas	10				10		
Team meetings to discuss investment ideas	15	5	5		5		
Money manager lunches and presentations	15	5	5		5		
Money manager research	10				10		
SMA* manager performance spreadsheet (monthly)	3				1	2	
MF manager performance spreadsheet (monthly)	3				1	2	
SMA* buy / sell monthly reports	5				1	4	

Specialist Structure Sample (continued)

Duty / Task	TEAM TOTAL	Advisor Name	Mktg Specialist Name	Est Plan Specialist Name	Stock Specialist Name	Tech Specialist Name	Admin Specialist Name
Investments - Individual Client							
Prepare current portfolio spreadsheets	34	4				30	
Maturing bond/GIC calls	24	8		8	8		
Stock trade calls	25	10			15		
Prepare individualized client spreadsheets	10					10	
Preparing recommendations	40				20	20	
Review recommendations with advisor	15	5			5	5	
Implementing / checking recommendations	30				10	20	
Financial Plans - Individual Client							
Gather data	5			5			
Input into financial planning software	10			10			
Create plan and associated graph	20			20			
Review plan	20	10		10			
Present plan to client	25	5		20			
Insurance - Individual Client							
Identify insurance opportunities / needs	8	2		6			
Prepare insurance quotes and recommendations	4			4			
Meet clients to review insurance proposals	8	2		6			
Premium reminder calls / e-mails	2			2			

Specialist Structure Sample (continued)

Duty / Task	TEAM TOTAL	Advisor Name	Mktg Specialist Name	Est Plan Specialist Name	Stock Specialist Name	Tech Specialist Name	Admin Specialist Name
Tax Return and Tax Strategy Services							
Tax loss selling	6	2		2	2		
Minimize tax impact: mutual fund year end distribution	2			2			
Tax package preparation	10			5		5	
Client gain / loss spreadsheets for taxes	10			5		5	
Admin - Group							
Sort mail	5						5
Filing	5						5
Identify incoming cash and securities	5						5
Review previous day transactions and revenue	15	5					10
Mutual fund trailers reconciliation	1						1
Review debit balances to find errors	2						2
Review credit balances for cash to invest	2						2
Restricted list follow-up (documents)	5						5
Monthly managed money fees (reconciliation)	3						3
Quarterly managed money fees (reconciliation)	3						3
Admin - Individual Client							
Opening new accounts / verify banking info	20						20
Updating KYCs	25		5				20
Documents and signing with advisor	8	4					4
Converting RRSPs into RRIFs	4						4
Requests sent to / from back office	20						20
Issue cheques / electronic funds transfer	10						10
Account transfers follow-up	10						10

Specialist Structure Sample (continued)

Duty / Task	TEAM TOTAL	Advisor Name	Mktg Specialist Name	Est Plan Specialist Name	Stock Specialist Name	Tech Specialist Name	Admin Specialist Name
Technology							
Various hardware problems / software problems	5					5	
Contact management system maintenance	1					1	
Design templates / macros	7	2				5	
Team Management							
Track team professional development (CE credits)	1					1	
Reconcile advisor pay statement (team payroll deductions)	2					2	
Payroll spreadsheet maintenance and bonus sheet	3					3	
Team meetings	30	5	5	5	5	5	5
Practice Analysis							
Daily incoming asset tracking	5						5
Revenue tracking by platform	1					1	
Monthly production and forecast spreadsheet update	1					1	
Update asset mix tracking spreadsheet (monthly)	1					1	
Monthly asset allocation / segmentation / mix	1					1	
Review of practice analysis reports	1	1					

*SMA - Separately Managed Accounts

<u>Acknowledgements</u>

My husband, Adrian Bannister, has been wonderfully encouraging and supportive of me in all my endeavours through the last 17 years of my career and the years it has taken me to write these handbooks. He has put up with my moods during stressful periods as an advisor, (the financial crisis comes to mind), as well as the trials and tribulations of my learning the process of writing and publishing these books. He has been a valuable sounding board and served as a test reader, editor and technical advisor. Adrian sometimes remembered important topics, issues and things I did during my career that I neglected to include in my early drafts. I feel very fortunate and thankful for his many contributions to my life and career.

I was extremely fortunate when a former associate of mine, Mike Bishop, agreed to work part-time with me to assist me with these books. He worked on my team for 18 years before I retired from my financial advice practice. Mike served as my editor, tech expert and sometimes as my memory and co-writer. I will be forever grateful for his help.

My practice's clients provided me with many of the ideas discussed in this book through their questions, requests and by sharing their life and business experiences with me. Thank you for all of your support and wonderful conversations throughout my career.

I have been very fortunate to draw upon many friends and contacts in the financial services industry while in the process of writing and publishing these handbooks. Many of these people served as test readers and editors, sometimes helping me to remember topics or issues that I needed to address in the books. Others simply provided much needed encouragement for me to share my experience and knowledge. I have listed the names in alphabetical order: Sonia Baxendale, John-Paul Bernardi, Rob Blagojevic, Laura Cameron,

Rose Cammareri, Sandy Cardy, Dianne Carruthers, Susan Carson, Jonathan Carter, James Collins, Cindy Crean, Megan Deeks, Wilma Ditchfield, Dan Downing, Stephen Dunn, Tim Eastwood, Carole Foster, Steve Geist, Monique Gravel, Rollie Guenette, Tony Johnson, Mark Kalichman, Katie Keir, Steven Krupika, Mara Ladico, Christine Lam, Grace Lutfy, Carol Lynde, Rod Mahrt, Paul Maranger, Gaelan Martin–Timms, Gary Mayzes, Jeff McCartney, B.K. Milne, Bruce Moore, Paul Musson, Katie Ophelders, Gabby Pulcini, Kevin Punshon, Jerry Rawlik, Meri Rawling-Taylor, Ann Richards, Tammie Rix, Stephanie Sienko, Mark Slater, Lois Smith, Sean Struthers, Iris Sugiyama, Rory Tufford, Timothy Tufford, Maili Wong.

Thanks to Ryan Levesque for his patience and advice while guiding me through the self publishing process.

Thanks to Melissa Levesque for her patience and help designing the covers and the formatting of the various forms of this handbook.

About the Author

Personal Background

Christine Timms was born into a family of small business owners, the youngest of five children all born within six years. She worked several part-time jobs as a teenager as she grew up in a small town in Southern Ontario, Canada. She put herself through university thanks, in large part, to the co-op work/study program at the University of Waterloo. Christine was always very competitive in sports, school and business, never shying away from a challenge. She is a lifelong fan of the Toronto Raptors, the Toronto Blue Jays, the Buffalo Bills and Canadian tennis players. Christine lives in Toronto, Canada with her husband and son.

Financial Services Career

As Christine began to understand herself more in the early years of her professional career, she realized that she needed to see a direct relationship between her efforts and success. She wanted to be her own boss and build her own business with no glass ceiling. She had always been curious about investing, was interested in teaching and enjoyed working with people. Christine wanted the freedom to think for herself and give independent advice to clients she could work with continuously over the life of her career. Christine had a competitive nature and sought an opportunity to be judged based on quantifiable results, effectively eliminating the glass ceiling. Christine determined the best opportunity to combine these interests and goals was through the career of a full-service investment advisor.

Christine was hired and trained by Merrill Lynch Canada in 1983. She began her career as an advisor with no clients after working for three years as an internal auditor for the Canadian Federal Government. She became an advisor at CIBC Wood Gundy when they bought Merrill Lynch Canada in 1990 and remained with CIBC Wood Gundy until retirement.

- Christine achieved chairman's club in her firm for the first time in 1993 and every year thereafter during her career (24 years in a row) including 2016, her last year as an advisor. Chairman's club included the top performers of the firm (usually approximately the top 8% of the firm's advisors).

- Christine served on CIBC Wood Gundy's Retail Advisory Board (committee of advisors assembled to provide feedback to firm management) from November 1995 to September 1999.

- Christine retired December 1, 2016 after 33 years as an investment advisor with career highs in both assets under management ($400 million) and annual revenue generated. Upon retirement, Christine's clientele consisted of about 350 households, with over a third of those households having over $1,000,000 in assets under management with Christine and her team. The clientele included people from all walks of life and occupations: professionals, small business owners, public service workers, skilled trade workers, retirees, widows, etc. Almost all clients were located in the Greater Toronto Area.

Educational History
1980 Bachelor of Mathematics (B. Math)
1982 Certified Management Accountant (CMA, CPA)
1983 Canadian Securities Course (CSC), options
1993 Chartered Investment Manager (CIM)
1995 Life Insurance and Accident & Sickness Insurance Licence
2000 Professional Financial Planning (PFP)
2010 Registered Retirement Consultant (RRC)
2015 Certified Executor Advisor (CEA)

Christine no longer holds any licence to practice as a financial advisor.

Books by Christine Timms

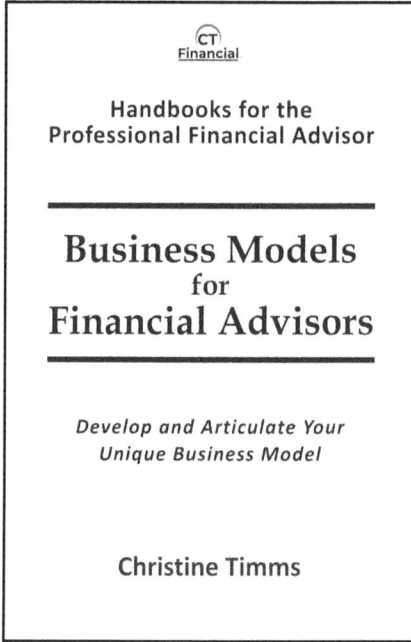

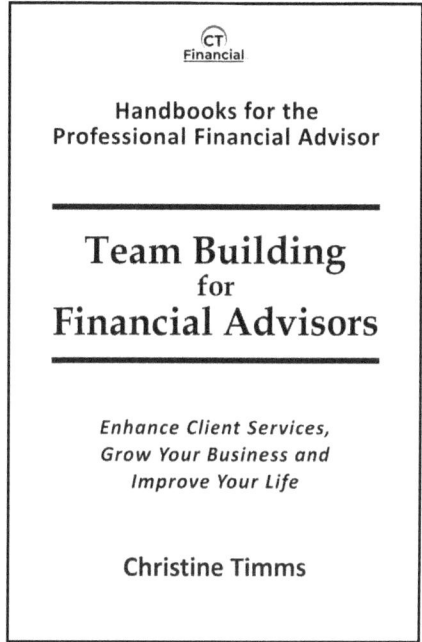

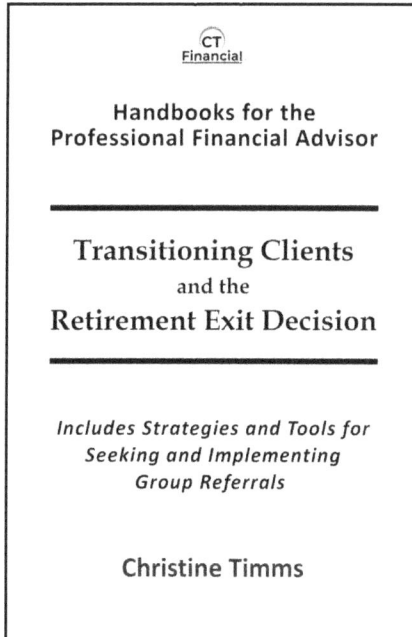

CT
Financial

**Handbooks for the
Professional Financial Advisor**

Business Models
for
Financial Advisors

---

*Develop and Articulate Your
Unique Business Model*

Christine Timms

CT
Financial

**Handbooks for the
Professional Financial Advisor**

Team Building
for
Financial Advisors

---

*Enhance Client Services,
Grow Your Business and
Improve Your Life*

Christine Timms

CT
Financial

**Handbooks for the
Professional Financial Advisor**

Transitioning Clients
and the
Retirement Exit Decision

---

*Includes Strategies and Tools for
Seeking and Implementing
Group Referrals*

Christine Timms

Templates Available on www.christinetimms.com

Business Models for Financial Advisors

Identify the Most Compatible Clients for Your Practice checklists
- Identify Compatible Groups of Clients and Potential Clients
- Identify Criteria for Sustainable Individual Relationships

Articulate Your Unique Service Model checklists
- Client Communication
- Investing
- Financial Planning
- Tax Strategies and Return Preparation

Determine Needed Resources and Suppliers checklists

Establish Pricing and Client Costs Model checklists

Choose Advisor Compensation Structure and Career Path checklists

Segmenting Clientele - Segmentation Criteria worksheet

Segmented Clientele Unique Service Model checklists

Client Investment Allocation Decision flow chart (free)

Team Building for Financial Advisors

Team Payroll Sensitivity Analysis spreadsheet

Advisor Actual Team Compensation Costs spreadsheet

Team Member Duty Distribution List - Associate Structure

Team Member Duty Distribution List - Specialist Structure

Transitioning Clients and the Retirement Exit Decision

Business Model Checklists (as shown in Business Models for Financial Advisors)

Steps of Transition Timeline checklist (free)

Potential Successor(s) Evaluation worksheet (free)

Sample Retirement Phone Call Script (free)

Sample Formal Retirement Letter (free)